Towards Economic Crisis (2012-2014) and Beyond

Towards Economic Crisis (2012-2014) and Beyond

ABOUT THE AUTHOR

As Chief Economic Advisor to the Government of India (1993-2001), **Shankar Acharya** was deeply involved in the economic reforms of the 1990s. He later served as a Member of the Prime Minister's Advisory Council (2001-2003) and the Twelfth Finance Commission (2004). Earlier he worked in the World Bank, where he led the World Development Report team for 1979 and was Research Adviser to the Bank. He has authored nine books and numerous scholarly articles.

Currently he is Honorary Professor at the Indian Council for Research on International Economic Relations (ICRIER) and serves on the boards of other research organisations, some corporates, charities and the Reserve Bank's Advisory Committee on Monetary Policy. He has a PhD from Harvard University and BA from Oxford.

Towards Economic Crisis (2012-2014) and Beyond

Shankar Acharya

ACADEMIC FOUNDATION
NEW DELHI

www.academicfoundation.org

First published in 2015
by

ACADEMIC FOUNDATION
4772-73 / 23 Bharat Ram Road, (23 Ansari Road),
Darya Ganj, New Delhi - 110 002 (India).
Phones : 23245001 / 02 / 03 / 04.
Fax : +91-11-23245005.
E-mail : books@academicfoundation.com
www.academicfoundation.org

Disclaimer:
The opinions/views/findings expressed in this book are solely those of the author and do not necessarily reflect the views of the publisher.

Acharya, Shankar N., author.
 Towards economic crisis (2012-2014) and beyond / Shankar Acharya.
  pages cm
 Essays originally published in the Business Standard over the period November 2011 to July 2015.
 Includes bibliographical references.
 ISBN 9789332703131

 1. Financial crises--India. 2. India--Economic conditions--21st century.   I. Title.

HC435.3.A24 2015   DDC 330.954   23

Typeset by Italics India, New Delhi.

Printed and bound by The Book Mint, New Delhi.
www.thebookmint.in

Contents

II
Crisis

III
Beyond Crisis

IV
General

Preface

The 39 essays in this volume were originally published in the *Business Standard* over the period November 2011 to July 2015. My thanks to that remarkable newspaper for allowing me include them in this volume.

In this digital age, in which good newspapers like the *Business Standard* allow a reader to access an author's current and past columns on their website quite easily, the obvious question that arises is what is the justification for collecting some of them in book form? Isn't it a somewhat redundant, and perhaps even vain, exercise? I asked these questions of my publisher. He assured me that there is still a "niche demand" for such volumes to make their publication economically viable. Apparently there are enough book buyers out there who still want to have ready access to a contributor's pieces in the old-fashioned book form. I still harbour doubts. But then I am not bearing the financial risk. As for the risk of royalties being meagre, I am fortunate enough not to rely on these volumes for a living.

So, to those select readers who still value the hard copy book form, my thanks in advance!

My warm thanks also to Rituraj Kapila for overseeing the production of this volume with his characteristic and enviable combination of courtesy, patience and professionalism.

— Shankar Acharya

Introduction

The essays in this volume cover the three and a half years between November 2011 and July 2015. For the Indian economy, this was a period of mounting economic malaise, bordering on crisis, up to early 2014, followed by a weak recovery since. These essays provide a month-by-month, contemporary account of this exceptionally difficult period of the country's post-1991 economic history. They also explore the factors which brought about the swift downfall from the heady years of high investment and rapid growth between 2003-04 and 2010-11 and outline the challenges in the way of resuming that earlier buoyant economic trajectory.

In the eight years, 2003-04 to 2010-11, economic growth averaged an unprecedented 8.5 per cent, despite the post-global-crisis dip below 7 per cent in 2008-09.[1] What's more, during the first five of these years, up to 2007-08, the Indian economy also showed excellent macroeconomic results in terms of low inflation, declining fiscal deficits and low external account deficits. After 2007-08, although economic growth regained momentum up to 2010-11, the other macroeconomic characteristics worsened 2008-09 onwards, with high inflation, growing external deficits and high fiscal deficits. These large macro imbalances were important reasons why the brief, post-2008-09 growth rebound proved unsustainable.[2]

By the end of 2011-12, economic growth had crashed from an annualised rate of 9 per cent in the last quarter of 2010-11 to just over 5 per cent in the final quarter of 2011-12. In the next two years, economic growth fell below 5 per cent, industry and employment

---

1. The GDP (gross domestic product) growth and national income data in this book relies on the 2000-2005 base series, partly because it was the only series available up through January 2015, partly because the new 2011-12 base series only provides growth estimates 2012-13 onwards and also because the data generated by the new series are still subject to vigorous controversy (see chapter 32).

2. A detailed account of these years is available in Acharya (2012a; 2012b).

stagnated but consumer price inflation stayed close to 10 per cent a year. The early chapters of the book detail the principal reasons for the collapse in growth and the even earlier deterioration in inflation, external deficits and fiscal imbalances. In summary, they include three sets of reasons: medium and long-term factors, short-term errors and weaknesses in policies and governance, and global economic conditions.

Among the most important long-term factors was the enormously disappointing absence of significant productivity-enhancing reforms since 2004, particularly in areas of labour laws, public sector banks, policy frameworks for key infrastructure sectors, agriculture, education, health and public administration. The United Progressive Alliance (UPA) government seemed content to coast on the high growth path of the mid-noughties and perhaps took it for granted, without appreciating that this mid-decade boom was a product of the accumulation of serious economic reforms carried out between 1991 and 2004 as well as an exceptionally buoyant world economy. With domestic reforms stalled and major industrialised economies reeling from the prolonged after-effects of the global financial crisis (2007-2009), India's growth momentum was bound to falter.

Second, the UPA government committed significant and avoidable policy and governance errors, including, most notably: a much delayed exit from the expansionary fiscal and monetary policies of 2008-09 (adopted to counter the downdraft from the global crisis); ramping up of several poorly designed, entitlement programmes (for rural employment, food security and education) without establishing the necessary revenue base; the tolerance of an overvalued exchange rate for the rupee; the non-adjustment of controlled prices for oil products, fertiliser and food in the face of the prolonged, China-fuelled, international commodity price boom until 2013, resulting in massive subsidies at the expense of public investment; the eruption of major scams in the allocation of telecom spectrum, coal blocks, other mining rights, land and various government contracts with lasting damage to the concerned sectors and the general quality of governance and administration; the encouragement of directed lending by public sector banks to a large portfolio of public-private infrastructure projects; the investor-confidence-destroying misadventure with retrospective taxation in the 2012 budget; and ham-handed tightening of environmental regulations, which further stalled major private and public projects.

All this substantially slowed economic growth, reduced investment and fuelled inflation, external deficits and fiscal imbalances. Confronted by the growing economic disarray, there was an attempt to restart reforms and restore fiscal prudence in late 2012 (see chapters 9 and 10). But it was a case of too little too late, exacerbated by the parliamentary opposition blocking some of the legislative changes. The economic slide continued, with the current account deficit in the balance of payments exceeding a record four per cent of GDP in 2011-12 and 2012-13 and triggering a sharp and disruptive depreciation of the currency in summer 2013, which had to be managed through a steep increase in policy interest rates, stringent controls on gold imports and a resort to high-priced, exchange guaranteed external borrowing. While a full-fledged balance of payments crisis was avoided, growth remained sluggish and inflation high. Furthermore, the 2013 crisis did not stop the government from enacting a near unworkable new land acquisition act, which raised major new barriers for both public and private investment. By spring 2014, as the country prepared for a national election, the economic malaise was deep and the legacy constraints on an early economic revival were severe (see chapters 22 and 23).

The general elections of April/May proved to be a watershed in political terms. After six years of double digit inflation and three years of slow growth, the UPA's core party, the Congress, was severely punished in the polls, garnering only 44 of the 542 Lok Sabha seats, while the UPA as a whole won 60 seats. The National Democratic Alliance (NDA) swept to power with 336 seats, with the Bharatiya Janata Party (BJP), led by Narendra Modi, alone winning 282 seats, thereby achieving the first single party majority in 30 years.

The Modi government's campaign promise of 'achhe din' (good days) was certainly appealing. But its first budget, presented six weeks after assuming power, did not set the Jamuna on fire. Instead of outlining a charter for radical reforms to spur economic revival, it seemed to convey much continuity with the preceding budgets and policies, dousing possibly exaggerated expectations of a sea change in economic policies (chapter 25).

However, as the year progressed, a successful strategy to contain inflation and push ahead with incremental reforms gradually took shape. By the end of the first year of the new government, these had cumulated to a fairly impressive package, including: the abolition of the subsidy on diesel; significant thrust to infrastructure investment, especially railways and highways; major expansion in the spread of household bank accounts (the Jan Dhan Yojana); deployment of this expanded platform to offer low-end life and accident insurance and a contributory pension scheme for unorganised workers; a sustained effort to amend the land acquisition act; growing support for labour policy reforms by states and centre; determined efforts to bring in the nation-wide Goods and Service Tax (in place of a large number of central and state, market-fragmenting levies) by April 2016; broadly successful auction of coal blocks earlier cancelled by the Supreme Court; amendment of the Mines and Minerals (Regulation and Development) Act to enable auctioning of licenses and promote non-coal mineral development; completing the long-pending amendment of insurance laws to lift the cap on foreign ownership from 26 to 49 per cent; and undertaking a serious effort to involve the private sector in defence production (chapter 33).

However, there was little progress in tackling some major policy problems. These included: the continuation of massive, wasteful and corruption-ridden subsidies to fertilisers and foodgrains, despite the potential of using the expanded bank account platform, the Aadhar unique identification system and the widespread mobile phone network to shift to much better targeted (and cheaper) systems of direct cash transfers; lack of a clear roadmap to tackle the serious problems of governance, performance and balance sheet weakness in public sector banks, coupled with a reluctance to reduce majority government ownership; little action in dealing with major distortions in the food economy, despite the analysis and recommendations of the Shanta Kumar Committee report; continuing problems with the inherited approach to PPP (public-private partnerships) in infrastructure development; tolerance of an over-valued exchange rate of the rupee to the detriment of exports and import-competing industries and sectors; avoidable errors in tax policy and administration, including the flip-flop on application of minimum alternative tax to foreign portfolio investors and the fresh enactment of an overly draconian new law against black money held abroad; and other continuing difficulties with significantly improving the investment climate.

Looking Ahead

In the early summer of 2015, the signs of economic recovery remain mixed and the outlook for an early return to sustained 8 per cent plus economic growth, along with robust expansion of job opportunities, remains clouded by both external and internal factors. Progress to date on the recent performance of these two key parameters remains bedevilled by the paucity of reliable data. In the case of employment, recent data is simply not available. For economic growth, that is growth in national output, data is available but of dubious validity.

This latter problem has arisen with the presentation, in January 2015, of national income data according to a new base of 2011-12, drawing on new and different data sources in key sectors. According to the new series, GDP grew at a little below 7.0 per cent in 2013-14 and a little faster than 7.0 per cent in 2014-15. In contrast, the old (2004-05 base) series had estimated growth at below 5 per cent in 2013-14 and around 5.5 per cent in the first half of 2014-15. The problem is that the new series estimates of higher growth for the two most recent years simply do not square with sluggish performance of all other economic indicators, such as corporate sales and earnings performance, tax revenues, bank credit, the industrial production index and piecemeal employment information (chapter 32). The overwhelming majority of knowledgeable observers of Indian economic developments agree that the current Indian economy simply does not 'feel' like one enjoying 7.0 per cent growth; 5.0-5.5 per cent seems much more believable.

Although the government has projected 8.5 per cent growth in 2015-16 (according to the new series), the Reserve Bank of India (RBI) expects growth at 7.6 per cent, in the light of the official, below-normal monsoon forecast, the continuing weaknesses in the global economy (especially Europe, China and Japan), the uncertainties relating to world energy prices and the subdued performance of various domestic economic indicators. That suggests that according to the old, now discontinued, national income series economic growth might not have exceeded 6 per cent. In other words, the performance of investment and growth in 2015-16 is likely to fall significantly short of the kind experienced in the boom of 2003-2011. On a more positive note, economic conditions do appear to be perceptibly better than in 2013-14 and gradually improving.

In the medium term, the global economy is unlikely to rebound strongly any time soon. The uncertainties with respect to Greece, the United Kingdom's continuation in the European Union, world energy prices, China's growth momentum and the timing of higher interest rates in the United States—all point against strong and sustained global growth. So, the acceleration of India's economic development will have to rely mainly on domestic factors, especially early success in reviving aggregate investment. This, in turn, will require continued fiscal prudence, a more competitive exchange rate, a substantially better investment climate and rapid progress in all the policy reform dimensions outlined above.

References

Acharya, Shankar (2012a). *India After the Global Crisis*. New Delhi: Orient BlackSwan.

————. (2012b). "India and the Global Crisis", in C. Fred Bergsten and C. Randall Henning (eds.), *Global Economics in Extraordinary Times*. Washington DC: Peterson Institute for International Economics.

I

Towards Crisis

1

Storm Clouds Over
the Economy

As autumn shades into winter, the clouds over India's economic performance and prospects are getting bigger and darker. First, the international economic climate is getting gloomier by the week, with a rising threat of a major 'event shock' from Europe. Second, India's economic growth has slowed and there is growing evidence that the deceleration will continue. Third, aggregate investment has slackened and it could get worse. Fourth, inflation continues to be stubbornly high, fuelled in part by a worsening fiscal deficit. Fifth, the country's external imbalances are growing at a time when capital flows are becoming more volatile. Sixth, and perhaps most worrying, there is little evidence that the government appreciates the gravity of the problems and even less that it has the capacity and the will to coordinate and implement an effective programme to mitigate the rising threats to economic performance. Each of these merits some elaboration.

Over the past few months, international economic news has been dominated by the extraordinary spectacle of European policymaking, if that's the right word to describe the seemingly never-ending circus of European summits, flawed bail-out agreements and subsequent back-sliding to cope with the witches' brew of sovereign fiscal stress, banking fragility and stalled growth. More than 18 months after the Greek fiscal crisis reared its ugly head, Europe is yet to find a lasting solution. What was manageable in the initial stages has spun increasingly out of control as European political will has lagged consistently and tragically behind economic necessity. Greece is stumbling in search of effective leadership, as is her far more important neighbour, Italy, bond markets are close to panicking, much of Europe has stopped growing (or is already in recession) and the durability of the eurozone is in serious doubt.

Unsurprisingly, successive editions of global economic projections, by the International Monetary Fund (IMF), Organization of Economic Cooperation and Development (OECD) and European Union (EU), foresee increasingly slower growth in the major economies of Europe, the United States (US) and Japan for the next couple of years and an even worse outcome if there is an event shock, such as a default on a European government's debt or a major bank failure. Some look hopefully to the BRICs—Brazil, Russia, India and China—for economic salvation for the world economy. But with nearly 60 per cent of the world economy (US, EU and Japan) hardly growing, it is surely unrealistic to expect the BRICs (with about 20% of global output) to provide the missing 'locomotive' role. Indeed, the opposite is more likely and is happening: the economic problems in the industrial world are pulling down the growth of exports, investment and output in the major emerging nations, including China and India. In short, near stagnation in the industrial world will continue to constrain India's growth potential for several years.

India's growth has been slowing over the past six quarters for this and several domestic reasons including: tightening supply constraints (because of a prolonged lack of effective reforms), rising interest rates, ham-handed implementation of environmental regulations and the succession of scams and scandals (notably in the allocation telecom spectrum, land, mining rights and some large government contracts), which have fuelled political acrimony and ground governmental decision-making to a virtual standstill. The latest data show that industrial growth slumped below 2 per cent (y-o-y) in September 2011, the lowest in many months. More ominously, some key service sector growth indicators have fallen sharply in April-July 2011 compared to April-July 2010: for example, cell phone connections to minus 31.0 per cent from plus 37.0 per cent; domestic air cargo traffic to minus 5.3 per cent from 33.6 per cent; and international air cargo traffic to 3.9 per cent from 25.3 per cent. HSBC's PMI (purchasing managers' index) for services fell to 49.0 per cent in October from above 60.0 per cent, eight months ago. Given that services (including construction) account for about 65.0 per cent of India's GDP, these trends are very worrisome.

Three months back, when government and the Reserve Bank of India (RBI) still expected economic growth in 2011-12 to be at 8.0 per cent or higher, I had predicted (*Business Standard,* 11 August 2011) GDP growth in the range of 7.0-7.5 per cent. Now that is looking a bit optimistic. There is a good chance growth could dip below 7.0 per cent.

Of perhaps greater concern is the growing evidence indicating a slowdown in investment. The growth of the key construction sector had slumped to 1.2 per cent in April-June 2011. Capital goods growth plummeted to minus 6.8 per cent in September. Project finance data from financial institutions shows a halving of the rate of commitments in the first few months of 2011-12 compared to the previous year. Numerous major projects are stalled or delayed due to regulatory setbacks and uncertainty relating to land acquisition, environmental rulings, cancelled coal linkages and so forth. Rising interest rates and falling corporate profits have tightened financial constraints on investment. Uncertainty over global economic conditions and a near paralysis in domestic governance casts a heavy pall over investment plans.

The outlook for production and investment is darkened by growing macro imbalances. The foreign trade deficit widened sharply in October to an unsustainable $20 billion; with the ratio of merchandise exports to imports dropping to barely 50.0 per cent for the first time since the 1980s. As the negative fallout from Europe grows and oil prices stay high (as most expect), external imbalances could easily worsen. Inflation remains stubbornly high, constraining the scope for investment-friendly monetary easing. The fiscal deficit is running well above budgeted levels, fuelling inflation and pushing benchmark 10-year government bonds close to 9.0 per cent. The banking sector is beginning to feel the stresses of a faltering economy. Debt restructurings and non-performing loans are on the rise. The situation will worsen as the credit cycle turns south. It's not a pretty picture.

The biggest and darkest cloud is the government's apparent failure to appreciate the gravity of the economic situation and take an effective step. Reforms, which should have been done long ago, could be initiated now. Untimely populist programmes could be shelved, or at least, postponed. Day-to-day administrative decision-making could be greatly improved. None of this is happening. And if the newspapers are to be believed, stasis is likely to continue from a weakened and fractured coalition government. But then let us be clear about the economic costs, which are already palpable. They will cumulate in the months ahead and further undermine investment, growth and macro stability. We could be in for several years of below 7.0 per cent growth; and worse if the Europe suffers a full-blown crisis.

15 November 2011.

2

Roosting Chickens, Building Crises

Nearly eight years have passed since the first United Progressive Alliance (UPA) government, led by Sonia Gandhi and Manmohan Singh, came to power. That's a long time in politics, long enough for many of the politically expedient sins of commission and omission to yield their unfortunate consequences. In the economic domain, the chickens have begun to come home to roost over the past year.

Consider the following potent brew of policy actions and non-actions:

- No significant economic reforms were carried out since 2004, with the honourable exception of the successful fiscal consolidation, which brought the combined (centre and states) deficit down from above 8.0 per cent of GDP (gross domestic product) in 2003-04 to 4.0 per cent in 2007-08 and helped fuel the savings and investment boom of that period. The lack of reforms has now slowed growth of productivity and output.

- That solitary major success was squandered in 2008 with massive subsidies for oil, fertilisers and food, the Sixth Pay Commission decisions, the farm loan waiver scheme and ramping up of the National Rural Employment Guarantee Programme (NREGP). The combined deficit more than doubled to 8.5 per cent of GDP, with the initial burst of populism cloaked by the later jargon of 'fiscal stimuli' to counter the global crisis of 2008-09. The deficit rose further to nearly 10 per cent of GDP in 2009-10 and has remained above 8 per cent, fuelling inflation and keeping longer-term interest rates high.

- This fiscal laxity has also placed the full burden of inflation-fighting in the last two years on monetary tightening by the

Reserve Bank of India (RBI), with consequent disproportionate damage to investment.

- The UPA's continued predilection for expanding entitlement programmes, such as the Right to Education Act and the Food Security Bill, do not augur well for fiscal correction in the near future. Incidentally, the former threatens closure of thousands of private primary schools, while the latter has been widely criticised for massive design flaws which may render it counter-productive.

- The other key, time-tested and successful macroeconomic policy of 'managing' the exchange rate of the rupee was abandoned after 2007, especially since 2009. The predictable (and predicted) result of unchecked rupee appreciation in the past two years has been soaring trade and CADs (current account deficits) since 2010, increase in external sector vulnerability, the costly shock of the steep depreciation of recent months and a significant drag on industrial growth.

- Since early 2008 world energy prices have increased sharply, with crude oil typically at or above $100 per barrel. The government has tried to suppress this hard fact by maintaining control over consumer prices of diesel, kerosene and LPG (liquified petroleum gas). Even the decontrol of petrol prices is not complete. The results have been huge subsidies (estimated at over one lakh crore in 2011-12) mostly to the better off, rampant adulteration of diesel and petrol, setback to energy conservation, discouragement of domestic oil and gas production and of alternative energy sources.

- The sluggish reforms in the coal sector, combined with the sudden promulgation of 'no go' areas in 2010, has shackled utilisation of India's most abundant energy resource, led to further strains on the rickety electric power sector and required much higher coal imports.

- The tightening of environment regulations in 2010 also hit high profile investment projects more generally, including major mining projects in Orissa, the Lavasa township project in Maharashtra and the Mundra port in Gujarat. This has clearly affected 'animal spirits' and investment adversely.

- Either due to 'coalition compulsions' or simply weak governance, massive irregularities and scams have been spawned in a number of sectors where the nexus of governmental discretionary decision-making and crony capitalism is high, including telecom licence and spectrum allocation, mining, Commonwealth Games projects, various land allocations and large government expenditure contracts. Subsequent discovery and scandal has been followed by widespread investigations and indictments and political mud-slinging, which, in turn, have contributed to a near stasis in normal administration and decision-making. Little wonder that entrepreneurial 'animal spirits' and investment intentions have been badly eroded.

- All this has taken its toll of India's resilient bounce-back from the global crisis of 2008-09. Economic growth has slumped from an annual rate of 8.9 per cent in 2010-11 second quarter to 6.9 per cent in the second quarter of 2011-12. With industrial production in October 2011 showing a contraction of 5.0 per cent, overall economic growth is expected to decelerate further in the second half of 2011-12. Worse, all indicators of investment (such as construction activity and capital goods production) are significantly negative. Economic growth in 2012-13 could easily be below 7.0 per cent; perhaps significantly below if Europe gets into a full-blown crisis.

With economic growth slowing below 7.0 per cent, the combined fiscal deficit still at a unsustainably high 8 per cent plus of GDP, headline inflation close to 9.0 per cent, the foreign trade (goods) deficit over 10.0 per cent of GDP, the CAD approaching 4.0 per cent of GDP, external commercial debt at a record high, capital inflows skittish and the global economic situation weak and uncertain (Europe on the brink? oil prices?), the macroeconomic signals are flashing red. Among the crises that are building are:

- An old-fashioned external liquidity crisis, perhaps precipitated by a European 'blow-out' or a surge in politically sensitive international oil prices. Given the overhang of maturing external debt and rising foreign scepticism about India's economic management capacities, our forex reserves of US\$ 300 billion may not suffice to tide us over an external shock, if fiscal policy continues to be profligate and reforms remain stalled. If we do get into such a crisis, it is going to be a lot harder to dig ourselves out than in the early 1990s.

- In the medium term, even if we can avoid an external payments crisis, lower investment levels and the sharpening constraints in energy, water and urban infrastructure could spawn a painful and drawn-out 'crisis' of several years of sub-seven per cent economic growth, well below the Twelfth Plan's aspirations of nine per cent, which could catalyse a number of economic, social and political vicious cycles.

- In the longer run, the continued absence of meaningful policies to increase substantially job opportunities (real jobs, not the make-work kind) for unskilled and semi-skilled labour in employment-intensive sectors is increasingly likely to convert the ongoing 'demographic dividend' of the youth bulge into a nightmare of unemployment, under-employment and social unrest.

- Such squandering of our development potential could profoundly weaken our national security in both the medium and long run. We live in a dangerous neighbourhood fraught with real threats and serious uncertainties and cannot afford such self-inflicted weakness.

12 January 2012.

3

Hope *versus* Experience

The setting: India's annualised economic growth rate has plummeted to 6 per cent in the final quarter of 2011, inflation is still stubbornly high, the CAD (current account deficit) in the BoP (balance of payments) exceeds 3.5 per cent of GDP (gross domestic product), external debt is at a record high, the fiscal deficit of the central government in the current year will exceed the budgeted level by at least ₹1 lakh crore, the aggregate investment rate in 2011-12 is officially estimated to have dropped by 4.0 per cent of GDP since 2007-08, the manufacturing sector has slowed to a crawl, mining output has fallen, the disinvestment programme is in disarray, capital markets are jittery and the international economic environment is weak and very uncertain. Two economists, Eternal Optimist (EO) and a somewhat older Consistent Realist (CR) are discussing what the forthcoming Union Budget might contain.

EO: This is it. This government has made such a mess of our economic policies, it is now bound to reverse course. Do you realise that our growth rate in the last quarter is almost as low as in the quarter after the Lehman bankruptcy in September 2008 at the peak of the global financial crisis? Now that the politicos have failed to deliver, they are bound to turn to the technocrats to save them from further embarrassment. You watch. This will be a historic budget, which will cut the fiscal deficit, revive economic reforms and reignite investment and economic growth.

CR: Really? What do you think the budget will do to vindicate your optimism? How can the fiscal deficit be reduced when subsidies are burgeoning and new (and poorly designed) entitlement programmes are being rolled out almost every year? Populism is hard to give up, even when it doesn't work. And what reforms do you think the budget will announce after so many years of doing very little?

EO: Just wait and see. They are going to allocate less money to the National Rural Employment Programme (NREP); they won't push the Food Security Bill, meanwhile they will raise the issue prices of foodgrains in the PDS (public delivery system); they will announce a credible programme for a phased increase in the prices of diesel, LPG and kerosene; they will raise the general rate for excise taxes, the CENVAT rate, and the rate on services by at least 2 per cent and move to a negative list; and they will restart the old programme of strategic sales (transferring controlling interest from the government to the private buyer). As for reforms…

CR: Hold on right there! Let's deal with this fiscal stuff first. It makes no difference what they allocate in the budget for NREP; the actual expenditures are determined by what happens in the states. And we know from painful experience that budget allocations for expenditure have little sanctity in recent years. The Food Security Bill will wind its own way through Parliament; we can only hope that the Standing Committee will rectify its obvious design flaws. But I wouldn't count on the opposition blocking the bill in the end. And a government which hasn't revised the issue price of PDS food for the last eight years isn't going to start now. As for raising all those petroleum distillate prices to bring them in line with high and rising international oil prices, I wonder what you have been smoking? Look, the government has even re-controlled (in practice) the freed up petrol price. I will only believe any 'credible programme' for petroleum price increases when they actually do them. Until then, we are stuck with huge energy subsidies and weakening oil companies. Strategic sales of PSUs (public sector undertakings)? Come off it. The same 'coalition compulsions' that blocked them for the last eight years will stymie them now, especially after the setback in the state elections. Now tell me about your reforms.

EO: Well, I believe the budget will quickly implement the GST (goods and services tax) reform and the DTC (direct taxes code). It will announce greatly expanded use of Aadhar to target beneficiaries of government programmes. The speech will herald revival of the stalled initiative to allow FDI (foreign direct investment) in multi-brand retail and increase the FDI limit for insurance. There will be significant reforms in agriculture. I also believe the budget speech will announce a reduction by the Reserve Bank of India (RBI) of interest rates to revive investment and growth. That will be a novel coordination of fiscal and monetary policy.

CR: You really must do better homework. The GST is stuck because of lack of political agreement between the government and the opposition and centre *versus* states. That's why the relevant Constitutional amending bill has been languishing for months. I foresee no early breakthrough. As for the DTC, the Standing Committee has recently reported on it. Perhaps it will be brought for debate in the House after the budget. Until one sees that version, it will be premature to assess how reformist it is. Remember that the whole exercise was started at a time of buoyant revenues, which is not our current condition. Greater use of Aadhar might well happen but I am less sanguine about an early revival of FDI in multi-brand retail. As for announcing an interest rate cut in the budget speech (which has happened in the 1990s), I doubt that the RBI will agree until it is confident about the credibility of the budget's fiscal consolidation effort. Incidentally, I notice you have given up on really important reforms like labour laws. Losing heart, EO?

EO: Come on, CR. How can you believe that the responsible government of a major nation will present a lacklustre, do-nothing budget when our economy is in such bad shape and going nowhere fast? Even you can't be that cynical.

CR: Not cynical my friend. Just someone whose hopes have been dashed by experience too many times. My advice: forecast on the basis of the government's track record...and be pleasantly surprised if one's minimalist expectations are exceeded.

---

9 March 2012.

4

The Unravelling

What a fall it has been my countrymen (and women). Four years ago India was riding high. We had just completed five unprecedented years of 9.0 per cent average annual growth. Poverty, we now know, had declined substantially, although that seems to displease most of our left-leaning political class (perhaps they think of the poor as vote banks?). Inflation had averaged hardly 5.0 per cent a year. The CAD (current account deficit) in the BoP (balance of payments) had averaged 0.5 per cent of GDP (gross domestic product). The combined (centre and states) fiscal deficit had come down to 4.0 per cent of GDP by 2007-08 from 9.0 per cent five years earlier. Aggregate investment had risen to a record high of 38.0 per cent of GDP. In international politics, the path-breaking civil nuclear deal had been signed and was soon to be validated in Parliament and then the Nuclear Suppliers Group in Vienna, marking a historic end to 34.0 years of nuclear and technological isolation. It reflected and enhanced our rising profile in global affairs. No wonder I dubbed these our "halcyon years" (*Business Standard,* 9 October 2008).

Look at us now. Economic growth has fallen to below 7.0 per cent. Industrial growth has collapsed. The aggregate investment rate has dropped to 34.0 per cent of GDP and is headed south, with many large projects stymied by problems of land acquisition, environmental roadblocks and a general policy stasis in government. Inflation has been near double digits for three years before moderating a bit in recent months. The CAD rose above 4.0 per cent of GDP, for the first time ever, in the final quarter of 2011 and is likely to be close to an unsustainable 4 per cent for the full year 2011-12. With exports having slowed, imports burgeoning, external debt at a new peak and capital inflows skittish, external stress is high and rising. The fiscal deficit and subsidies are, frankly, out of control. The centre alone showed a deficit of 6.0 per cent of GDP in 2011-12 and, with states, the combined deficit is likely to be close to 9.0 per cent, as it has been in the previous three fiscally profligate years.

Nor does last month's budget hold out credible hopes for a reversal of our macroeconomic woes. The budget's promise of a modest fiscal correction (less than 1.0% of GDP) in 2012-13 is critically dependent on reducing the massive subsidies for petroleum products, fertilisers and food. All of these entail substantial (and long overdue) increases in their controlled prices. That certainly looks dicey given Mamata Banerjee's well-known opposition to price increases, and her demonstrated capacity for making the central government reverse course: recall the serial capitulations over the Teesta waters agreement with Bangladesh, FDI in multi-brand retail and, most recently, the debacle over the Railway budget and change of minister. Nor is the budget likely to ignite animal spirits for investment, given its damaging proclivity for 'retroactivitis' in tax policy and major expansion of administrative discretion in large swathes of tax administration.

The disarray in policy and performance is not limited to the economic domain. After the prolonged and bizarre legal tussle over the army chief's birth date, last month saw disclosures of attempted bribing of the chief by a recently retired general over a defence contract and the puzzling decision by the chief and the defence minister not to pursue the matter. Then came news of strange unauthorised movements of military units towards Delhi in January, which were reportedly taken very seriously by the civilian establishment. Perhaps even more damaging was the army chief's leaked recent letter to the prime minister warning of systemic defence unpreparedness in key areas, including tank ammunition supply, artillery and air defence. If the contents of the letter were seriously inaccurate, how does the army chief still retain the confidence of the government? And if the letter describes a distressing reality of military unpreparedness for lack of supplies and equipment, then that responsibility rests with the Gandhi-Singh government of the last eight years, especially its defence minister.

In his damning, recent article, the highly respected doyen of Indian journalism, George Verghese, has written (*Business Standard*, 3 April 2012), "The disgraceful civil-military crisis India has witnessed denotes complete failure of leadership on the part of the army chief and the defence minister." He goes on to write: "The larger and far more important issue that must be addressed is the dismaying exhibition of deep systemic and structural rot...Indecision, drift and factionalism, not just on defence issues, have become the hallmarks of governance and politics." He might have added a reference to the explosive growth in corruption over the past decade, which is now spilling out in the open in many areas, especially those where governmental control and discretion in allocating economic resources remains high. The tragic irony is that despite the unquestioned probity of the prime minister, this government is widely believed to have presided over an unprecedented expansion of corruption in India.

Many strands of history, politics and economics have led to today's sorry state of national affairs. An important one must surely be the novel and peculiar structure of post-2003 governance where the prime minister has been appointed by the head of the dominant party in the ruling coalition and has little, if any, authority over his cabinet colleagues. The Westminster model of parliamentary democracy depends critically on the prime minister's power to appoint and sack his ministers. Manmohan Singh has clearly lacked that crucial authority, which has been wielded by the Congress president, Sonia Gandhi. So, as many have noted, he has the formal responsibility for the government's actions but is bereft of real political power. She has the power but not the responsibility. After eight long years, it is painfully evident that this peculiar form of diarchy has served India ill. It has utterly undermined the principle of cabinet responsibility. Ministers have felt free to run their ministries as autonomous fiefdoms. The less scrupulous have exploited such freedom to extort huge rents from governmental decisions in their domain. And let the devil take the hindmost, in this case the people of India and their collective national interest.

So where do go from here? There is no silver bullet. Ultimately, in a democracy, people get the government they elect. Some say they get the one they deserve! I hope we Indians deserve better...

---

12 April 2012.

5

The Exchange Rate
Economics Bites Back

Since last August the Indian rupee has been volatile and weak. The rupee-dollar parity dropped from around 44-46 in the summer of 2011 to a low of 54.2 in mid-December. Some regulatory measures and substantial market intervention by the Reserve Bank of India (RBI) in December and January (about $ 8 billion of dollar sales each month) restored the rate to around 50 by end January. After the presentation of the Union Budget in mid-March 2012, the rupee has been again jittery and anaemic, dropping to an all-time low of 54.9 on 18 May, raising serious concerns in both media and Parliament. Senior government spokesmen have frequently blamed the unfolding Greco-European crisis as the principal cause for the rupee's woes. That is certainly an important factor but almost certainly not the dominant one.

The real cause of the rupee's weakness is the relentless deterioration of our economic policies in recent years. A falling rupee is simply a symptom of the underlying disease: unsound economic policies. After hovering around 1.0 per cent of GDP (gross domestic product) or less since 1991-92, the CAD (current account deficit) in our BoP (balance of payments) exceeded 2.5 per cent of GDP in 2009-10 and 2010-11 and is likely to have swelled to a new high of 4.0 per cent in 2011-12. The combined (centre and states) fiscal deficit more than doubled from its post-consolidation low of 4.0 per cent of GDP in 2007-08 to 9.0 per cent in 2008-09, and remained above 8.0 per cent in the next three years, despite governmental promises of exit from expansionary (read populist) fiscal policies. Inflation has been stubbornly high for three years and counting. Investment rates have fallen and may drop further. Sectoral problems and constraints have proliferated; just think of power, telecom, oil and gas, fertilisers, airlines and textiles, to mention a few.

None of this was either preordained or unavoidable. They reflect prolonged disarray, indecision (and sometimes corruption) and political 'compulsion' (a kind of revealed preference) in favour of soft options. To take an example, the continuation of high fiscal deficits after 2009-10 cannot be justified as necessary antidote to global economic problems. Rather it reflected failure to check rapidly increasing subsidies for oil products, fertilisers, foodgrains and electricity, and a clear political preference for launching and expanding entitlement programmes (sometimes of dubious efficacy) without assuring their fiscal and economic sustainability. Similarly, the steadily worsening finances of key government controlled enterprises, such as railways, power utilities, oil companies, the government coal company and the national airline reflect deep-seated preference for political expediency over economic and commercial good sense. Even the major success story of mobile telephony has become vulnerable to the compromise and sleaze associated with 'coalition compulsions'.

There have also been non-political policy errors. For example, in the period between spring 2009 and summer 2010, as world trade and capital flows recovered after the global crisis, the Reserve Bank of India (RBI) chose to allow the steepest ever appreciation of the rupee: about 15 per cent in terms of the 36-currency, trade-weighted REER (real effective exchange rate) index and over 20 per cent according to the 6-currency REER index relating to major trading partners. As I pointed out in a series of articles in *Business Standard* in 2010 (10 and 22 April, 23 September and 25 November), this steep appreciation of the rupee made little sense against the background of widening trade and current account deficits. The better policy would have been to moderate the appreciation through reserve-augmenting dollar purchases by the RBI along the lines it so successfully deployed in 2003-2007. This would have reduced the level of external deficits we are now facing, increased the war-chest of forex reserves and contained the damage to our industrial growth from weakened competiveness.

However, the primary responsibility for worsening economic policies clearly lies with government and includes: the costly tightening of environmental regulations in 2010, which hit major completed and ongoing projects and sharply curtailed areas for coal mining; and the proliferation of major scams in the allocation of government-controlled resources (such as telecom spectrum) and their aftermath of near stasis in governmental decision-making with adverse consequences for the investment climate.

Against the darkening background of deteriorating economic policies and outcomes, there were hopes that the 2012-13 budget would point to a brighter future. Such hopes were dashed in mid-March when the budget presented a lurch towards retrospective taxation, an expansion of discretionary authority of tax administration and little by way of credible measures to tackle the yawning fiscal deficit. Small wonder that investor sentiments, both domestic and foreign, suffered a major setback. The resulting slowdown in net foreign capital inflows contributed to recent declines in the rupee's value.

Basically, the rupee's exchange rate is acting as both a shock-absorber and a warning to policymakers to improve the coherence and rationality of our economic policies. A depreciated rupee is also acting as a built-in stabiliser by cheapening Indian assets (and thus encouraging dollar inflows) and making exports and import-substituting activities more profitable. So, in theory, a cheaper rupee should, in time, improve both the current and capital accounts of our external finances. But sharp and unexpected depreciations can also be excessive and destabilising. So, the RBI is, quite correctly, trying to put some brakes on the process, even though market intervention in turbulent times is more an art than a science. However, RBI actions are palliatives, at best. The real cure lies with the government's economic policies.

So what should be done? When a senior public official asked me that recently, my somewhat unhelpful response was "I wouldn't like to start from where we are today!" More constructively, the first order of business should be to bite that promised bullet and raise petroleum and fertiliser prices to reduce the burgeoning subsidies. Second, the government should undertake administrative steps to implement some mood-lifting reforms. Whether this relates to FDI (foreign direct investment) in retail or some other measures, the authorities are best positioned to judge what is feasible. Third, the government should focus on debottlenecking large, ongoing public and private projects. Fourth, the government should accelerate efforts to achieve agreement with the opposition parties and states to implement the long-promised GST (goods and services tax). Finally, the government and the RBI should work out contingency measures to deal with the consequences of further turbulence (including possible break-up) of the eurozone.

Even a modest improvement in economic policies, together with some luck on global oil prices could improve our economic prospects. In their absence, we are in for a difficult time. As the old adage goes: "what can't go on, won't".

---

21 May 2012.

6

Half Full or Three-Quarters Empty?

By now everyone is familiar (unless they have been holidaying in Mars) with the litany of bad news on India's economic performance in the past year: growth sharply down, industry in doldrums, inflation still uncomfortably high, fiscal deficits bloated by seemingly uncontrollable subsidies, external imbalances at record levels, investment climate gloomy, policy stasis continuing...and so on. Nevertheless, looking ahead, the future prospects are not necessarily of unrelieved gloom. It is possible to construct plausible alternative scenarios: one moderately positive, another more relentlessly negative.

Let us start with the positive first, the one that finds ready support from various senior government spokesmen. The ingredients include:

- The global economic situation looks better than a few months back. The US economy is still growing, even though slowly. Europe seems to be coming to grips with her underlying problems and there is a real chance that although growth will remain anaemic, a full-blown euro-crisis will be avoided.

- Sluggish industrial country growth (and a little slower growth in China) will continue to moderate commodity prices, especially oil, which has been mostly below \$100/bbl in recent months. Lower oil and gold prices will help reduce India's external deficits.

- Despite short-term economic weaknesses, India's long-term growth drivers of a youthful demography, technological 'catch up' and demonstrated entrepreneurial talent remain in play. Further, the official national accounts still point to an aggregate investment rate of 35.0 per cent of GDP (gross domestic product) in 2011-12. This suggests that the current growth slowdown may be temporary, reflecting mainly global economic problems.

- The 20.0 per cent or so depreciation of the rupee in the past year should help correct current and capital account imbalances as time passes. This substantial devaluation should also spur industrial and services activity for both exports and import substitution.

- Since the takeover of the finance portfolio by the PM (Prime Minister) a fortnight back, various senior government figures from the PM down have at last acknowledged the gravity of our economic problems and talked up a variety of likely policy changes/reforms including: dilution of the General Anti-Avoidance Rule (GAAR), some rollback of retrospective tax measures adopted in the March budget, significant increases in petroleum prices to reduce subsidies, revival of proposals for FDI (foreign direct investment) in multi-brand retail and aviation, legislative progress on pension and insurance bills, rapid progress on the GST (goods and services tax), coordinated efforts to debottleneck major infrastructure projects, and other efforts to improve the investment climate. Much of this is expected to happen after the President's election is over.

- Furthermore, to ensure the political feasibility of these necessary policy changes, moves are afoot to realign the government's political base by forming issue-based partnerships with the Samajwadi party and others, and thus finesse Mamata Banerji's oft-demonstrated veto.

- Finally, the positive scenario draws strength from a number of accounts of strong, state-level economic progress and suggests that reforms and performance in states will contribute increasingly to the overall India development story.

So much for the positive story, which sees economic growth reviving to 7.0 per cent this year and perhaps 8.0 per cent in 2013-14. The alternative, more negative view runs as follows:

- The global economic situation is still uncertain, with the European crisis far from resolved. Event shocks can still happen and if they do, the damage to India could be significant.

- India's long-term growth drivers may be present, but their positive influence seems to have been outweighed by too many years of bad economic policies.

- It is unrealistic to expect a sudden resuscitation of good economic policies just because the PM has taken over the finance portfolio. He may be able to dilute the damage inflicted by the March budget. But the political feasibility of urgently needed administered price increases and the oft-listed raft of reform measures remain debatable. There may be some progress but much less than the optimists expect. After all, it was the same PM and the same United Progressive Alliance (UPA) government presiding over the past eight years of non-reform.

- Furthermore, the damage inflicted by the last three years of corruption scandals and the associated policy stasis is not easy to reverse, when it comes to reenergising the administrative machinery to resolve problems of land acquisition, environmental clearances, fuel supply linkages, inter-sectoral coordination and various other hurdles to swifter project implementation. This is specially so when long overdue administrative reforms have not been implemented.

- Some of India's states are clearly doing better than others. And that is very welcome. But when one considers some of the key sectors where states have primary responsibility, such as power distribution/pricing, agricultural research and extension, urban development, primary and secondary education and healthcare and overall governance, the performance is generally quite unsatisfactory with very few good outliers. So the states may not serve as major reform engines of the future.

- In the current year, 2012-13, let alone 7.0 per cent economic growth, even 6.0 per cent may become a bar too high if the monsoon fails. The chances of that are now quite significant, given the massive rainfall deficiencies up through the first week of July.

- As for the near future, the dismal performance of industry in the past year, coupled with signs of slowdown in services, make the prospects for a return to 8.0 per cent plus growth look increasingly dim.

- Quite apart from short-term growth prospects, the medium-term challenges of creating manufacturing jobs for the burgeoning labour force and providing viable structures of urban governance and finance to a rapidly urbanising population seem quite daunting, especially given the record of weak performance to date. For example, significant chunks of labour-using manufacturing have been relocating out of East Asia as wages rise there. But the preferred destinations continue to be countries like Bangladesh and Vietnam, not India. Apparently, employment-friendly labour laws, basic skill endowments, infrastructure and investment climate offer a better package in those nations than we can.

So how does the glass look? You can take your pick. On present trends, the three-quarters empty scenario looks more plausible to me. Who knows, perhaps a strong burst of policy reform after the Presidential election will confound my expectations.

---

12 July 2012.

7

Crises Still Building

At the beginning of 2012, I had pointed out that because of the United Progressive Alliance (UPA) government's prolonged lack of progress on economic reforms, continued fiscal profligacy, a series of damaging decisions injurious to the investment climate and a weak and uncertain global economic environment, a number of crises were building (Chapter 2: "Roosting Chickens, Building Crises"). Four were specifically outlined: "an old-fashioned external liquidity crisis"; "a painful and drawn-out crisis of several years of sub-seven per cent economic growth"; a lack of jobs for unskilled and semi-skilled labour, which might convert "the ongoing …youth bulge into a nightmare of unemployment, under-employment and social unrest"; and, consequent "on such squandering of our development potential", the weakening of "our national security in the medium and long run". Now, more than seven months later, it may be instructive to assess what progress, if any, the Gandhi-Singh government has made in warding off these premonitions of crises.

We have already had a foretaste of external liquidity pressures in two bouts of sharp exchange rate depreciation, the most recent of which was in the weeks after the retrograde March budget, which took the rupee/dollar parity to around 56, where it has hovered since, compared to the rate of 44-45 a year ago. This sharp nominal depreciation of about 25 per cent is both a reflection of external liquidity pressures and a means of encouraging improvement in our current and capital accounts. Cheaper rupee assets, some progress in resolving the eurozone crisis and renewed hopes of fiscal corrections and reform actions by the Indian government appear to have helped attract strong inflows of foreign portfolio investment, which have eased the financing of the large CAD (current account deficit) and supported the rupee at present levels.

But after two changes in finance ministers and a diet of brave words but little by way of long-promised, bullet-biting actions, especially on the crucial issue of diesel price increases, hopes may again be fading. External credit rating agencies have placed India on a negative outlook for a downgrade from investment grade and external debt markets for Indian paper are already pricing them near junk status. With its economy contracting, the eurozone continues to be fraught with high risk, and the possibility of a highly destabilising Israeli attack on Iran remains substantial. Recent data show a decline in Indian exports in the first quarter of 2012-13 and a further deterioration of our external debt profile. The Prime Minister's Economic Advisory Council (PMEAC) projects a CAD of almost 4 per cent of GDP (gross domestic product) in 2012-13 in its latest *Economic Outlook*. In short, our external finances remain very vulnerable to shocks and swings in sentiment. The longer we postpone overdue petroleum product price increases and growth-enhancing policy actions, the higher the chance of renewed external pressure and another disruptive tumble in the rupee's value.

And this time it may prove harder to manage and contain the collateral economic damage of a sudden depreciation, since the domestic financial system is now clearly stressed by rising levels of non-performing and restructured loans to a growing number of sizeable companies, especially in power, telecom, real estate and mining sectors.

As for the medium-term crisis of low (sub-7.0%) growth, we are now well into the second year. The rapid deceleration during 2011-12 saw the quarterly growth rate plummet from above 9.0 per cent in the last quarter of 2010-11 to 5.3 per cent in the final quarter of 2011-12, yielding an average growth for the full year, 2011-12, of 6.5 per cent, the lowest in nine years. With the index of industrial production showing no growth in the first quarter of 2012-13 (down by 0.7 per cent for manufacturing) and the weak monsoon suggesting little growth in agriculture (the otherwise optimistic *Economic Outlook* projects 0.5 per cent for 2012-13), most independent analysts and forecasters foresee GDP growth to be below 6 per cent in 2012-13. It is hard to reconcile the currently known facts and data about the economy with the Prime Minister's Independence Day speech expectation of 'a little more' than 6.5 per cent. The more recently published *Economic Outlook* projects 6.7 per cent, but its associated forecasts of 5.3 per cent for industry and 8.9 per cent for services seem very optimistic.

Some people have trouble reconciling India's 35.5 per cent ratio of aggregate investment to GDP in 2011-12 with her current low rates of growth. Earlier this month, the prime minister also was reported to have drawn comfort from India being "a high savings, high investment economy." But consider the following points. First, the aggregate savings rate has declined from a peak of 37.0 per cent of GDP in 2007-08 to 31.0 per cent in 2011-12, thanks mainly to high central government revenue deficits and lower corporate profits. Second, the aggregate investment rate includes the recent increases in stocks of privately-held gold and publicly-held foodgrains, neither of which contributes noticeably to output. If one focuses on ratio of gross fixed investment to GDP, that ratio has fallen from its peak of 33.0 per cent in 2007-08 to about 28.0 per cent in the second half of 2011-12. Third, the aggregate investment data includes spending on projects, quite a few of which have been stalled since 2010 because of tighter environmental constraints, scams, court judgements and other impediments. They also include the costly investment in around 25,000-30,000 megawatts of mostly new power generation capacity, now standing idle because of absent linkages to coal or gas, or because near-bankrupt state distributing companies lack the money to purchase their power.

Until these critical infrastructure bottlenecks are sorted out, and there is a marked improvement in fiscal imbalances, the investment climate and financial sector health, it is hard to see how India's growth can break out of its current 5-7 per cent band. The economic and social welfare losses of such avoidably low growth are massive.

The third crisis of growing scarcity of jobs for the 'youth bulge', the vast majority of whom lack usable skills, has been building over decades and has clearly got worse with the slowdown in economic growth, especially in labour-intensive manufacturing. The recent increase in industrial disputes, sectarian strife and other social stresses has multiple causes, including the worsening shortage of decent employment opportunities.

Finally, it was heartening to hear the Prime Minister, in his Independence Day address, draw attention to the strong link between our sustained economic progress and our national security. That security has clearly been weakened by our faltering economic performance. Equally clearly, it can only be restored and enhanced when our government and politics work to implement sensible, growth-promoting economic policies.

---

27 August 2012.

8

Macro Signals Flashing Red

It is common knowledge that the Indian economy has not just been doing badly for over a year but is actually stumbling towards a major economic crisis. The government seems incapable of remedial action, punch-drunk by successive scams, political weakness, internal incoherence and perhaps even sheer incompetence. It's beginning to feel like a classic tragedy where a nasty end seems increasingly unavoidable. All that an external observer can do is record the painful journey. The macroeconomic data that has emerged over the past couple of weeks or so all point to a worsening situation.

Economic Growth

We now know that economic growth in April-June 2012 was 5.5 per cent, meaning that in the first half of calendar 2012 India grew at 5.4 per cent, far below the 8.4 per cent rate of 2009-10 and 2010-11, not to mention the 9.0 per cent average of 2003-2008 and an initial aspiration of 9.0 per cent plus for the Twelfth Plan period. In fact, news reports that the Planning Commission is debating a revised target growth in the range of 8.2-9.0 per cent for the Twelfth Plan appear sadly laughable in the current context.

Furthermore, the data for the first half of 2012 show no growth in manufacturing, barely 2.0 per cent in mining and 2.3 per cent in agriculture. With such low growth in the main commodity sectors, it is difficult to understand how service sectors such as construction, finance and business services continue to record double-digit growth rates. Who knows, perhaps all the numbers will be significantly revised in a few months!

External Sector

More than a month back, the Reserve Bank of India (RBI) informed us that India's CAD (current account deficit) in her BoP (balance of payments) had swelled to a record high of 4.2 per cent of GDP (gross domestic product) in 2011-12, a major reason behind the substantial depreciation of the rupee over the past year. Last week the commerce department released the latest trade data for July 2012, which show the dollar value of merchandise exports plummeting by 15 per cent compared to a year before. Imports also fell but at half that rate, yielding an uncomfortably high July trade deficit of over $ 15 billion. All this is consistent with our slippage in global competitiveness as ranked by the latest report of the World Economic Forum.

With growing likelihood of further quantitative easing in monetary policy in the United States (US) and Europe, some may feel that capital inflows into India will increase sufficiently to finance our large trade and current account deficits. Maybe. But the disarray in our real economy and policies is discouraging FDI (foreign direct investment) and Indian equity markets look less attractive to foreign portfolio investors than quite a few other possible destinations. A possible downgrade by major credit rating agencies would compound the problem. Furthermore, looser monetary policy in US and Europe could be a mixed blessing for India, as it might drive up commodity prices, especially of oil and gold, thus swelling Indian imports and fiscal deficits.

This week's release of India's external debt data by the finance ministry shows a further deterioration of key debt ratios by March 2012. Nothing dramatic, but the trend is clearly negative, and warns against the growing recourse to external debt finance. Taken together, the latest information points to a further increase in our external vulnerability at a time when our policy capacity to deal with unexpected shocks is manifestly low.

Fiscal Imbalance

Fiscal profligacy is alive and kicking. A few days back the Controller General of Accounts (CGA, not CAG! [Comptroller and Auditor General]) informed us that the central government's fiscal deficit for the first four months of 2012-13 had already exceeded half of the full year budget target. More recently, there are ominous, if unsurprising, indications of a significant deceleration in direct tax collections up though August, especially from companies, with gross corporate tax revenues stagnant compared to April-August of the previous financial year. Despite finance ministry reassurances, tax collections for the year could fall significantly below budget targets because of sluggish economic activity.

The real fiscal spoilsport is, of course, subsidies, especially those for diesel, LPG (liquified petroleum gas) and kerosene, though those on fertiliser and foodgrains are also large. Data circulated by the petroleum ministry indicate under-recoveries by OMCs (oil marketing companies) of ₹17/litre on diesel, ₹33/litre on kerosene and ₹347/cylinder on LPG. At current prices, total under-recoveries are estimated at around ₹190,000 crore or almost 2 per cent of GDP. Even allowing for 'contributions' by upstream public oil majors, the burden on the budget is likely to be several times the budget provision of ₹40,000 crore. Unless the controlled prices are raised. That obvious and rational expectation has been confounded many times since the last increase in June 2011. Even if there are some price increases, the issue remains of how much. Token increases will not solve the giant problem. The failure to push through substantial increases will not only entail a large slippage in the fiscal deficit (and hence in the government's already massive borrowing requirements), but could also jeopardise the OMCs' operational ability to maintain adequate supplies of key distillates, with obvious and substantial negative consequences.

Financial Sector

As economic and industrial growths have slowed, financial stress has risen. The NPAs (non-performing assets) of banks have grown, as have recourse to restructuring of loans by many corporate borrowers. A fortnight back, Credit Suisse released a report pointing to the high and increasing level of concentration in bank borrowers, with 10 groups accounting for 13.0 per cent of all bank loans (compare 1.0% by top 10 companies in China and 5.0% in Korea) and receiving over 20.0 per cent of the increment in bank lending in 2011-12. Furthermore, these 10 big borrowers are also concentrated sectorally, mainly in power, mining and metals, areas with well-known special problems. Banking vulnerability has clearly increased.

Inflation

Although headline WPI (wholesale price index) inflation dipped marginally below 7.0 per cent in July 2012 for the first time in three years, the CPI (consumer price index) rate of inflation remained close to 10.0 per cent. So the problem of low growth coexisting with high inflation persists, reducing the probability of early and significant reductions in policy interest rates by the RBI.

Employment

India does not have reliable, current data on employment. But what little information is available shows unfavourable trends. Thus, a recent survey by The Associated Chambers of Commerce & Industry of India (ASSOCHAM), reported in the latest *India Today*, shows substantial slowdowns in the growth of jobs in the urban, formal sector in April-June 2012 compared to the preceding quarter: by 31.0 per cent in IT (information technology) services, 29.0 per cent in hospitality, 12.0 per cent in banking and financial services, 19.0 per cent in automobile manufacture, 26.0 per cent in engineering, 20.0 per cent in infrastructure and construction, and so on. Similar results emerge from Federation of Indian Chambers of Commerce and Industry's (FICCI) business confidence survey for April-June 2012: over four-fifth of the 150 companies surveyed expected their hiring to decline or remain unchanged.

So, every macro indicator for the economy is flashing red, while we wait for the government to undertake serious corrective policies.

---

13 September 2012.

9

Reforms Resurgent?

My column "Macro Signals Flashing Red" (Chapter 8), highlighted the continuing and dangerous deterioration in our economic performance with respect to economic growth, external sector imbalances, fiscal deficit, financial sector stresses, inflation and employment. As if on cue, that evening the government announced a ₹5/litre increase in diesel prices and capped the number of subsidised LPG cylinders a household could receive at six per year. The next day the government announced a set of reform measures, including opening up to FDI (foreign direct investment) in multi-brand retail and domestic civil aviation. Despite a week of high decibel opposition from various political parties and the exit of the Trinamool Congress from the United Progressive Alliance (UPA) coalition, the government held firm on its decisions.

In subsequent weeks, there have been clear signs that the General Anti-Avoidance Rules (GAAR) proposed in the March budget would be postponed by three years and the retrospective tax measures deployed in that budget would be reviewed. A complex scheme for resolving state electricity dues has been put in place. Last week the government followed up with cabinet approval of a slew of legislative reforms, including the Insurance Amendment bill (with FDI cap raised to 49.0%), the long pending Pensions bill and Companies Amendment bill, the Forward Contracts (Regulation) Amendment bill, and amendments to the Competition Act. Cabinet also formally approved the Twelfth Plan. A National Investment Board may soon be announced also.

The sudden emergence of the government from somnolence and policy stasis to near frenetic activity has undoubtedly improved short-term expectations substantially, catalysing around $4 billion of equity market inflows (net) by FII (foreign institutional investors), lifting the Sensex by nearly 10.0 per cent and strengthening the rupee by about

8.0 per cent against the US dollar. The dire warnings of an imminent downgrade by major rating agencies have receded, the pink papers are replete with 'big bang reform' headlines and spokesmen for industry are buoyant. What should one make of all this? Are we really launched on a reforms-fuelled burst of growth and superior macroeconomic performance of the kind we enjoyed in 1992-1997 and 2003-2008? Let us attempt a sober assessment.

First, on the fiscal front, at mid-September prices, the diesel and LPG (liquified petroleum gas) measures will probably reduce the Centre's subsidy bill by about 0.2 per cent of GDP (gross domestic product), from around 2.6 per cent of GDP estimated by the recent Kelkar Committee report, leaving the expected total well above the March budget's desired 'cap' of 2.0 per cent of GDP. The Kelkar report recommends increases in the issue price of foodgrains from public stocks in line with increases in minimum support prices, full decontrol of sugar, a 10.0 per cent increase in urea with annual cost-related adjustments to follow and a go-slow on the Food Security Bill. The report also recommends a new system to accelerate disinvestment and cuts in Plan expenditure. None of this looks imminent. In that case, the Centre's fiscal deficit is likely to be at least 0.5 per cent of GDP higher than the 5.1 per cent budgeted, and the combined deficit (centre plus states) close to 8.0 per cent of GDP. In short, the petroleum price measures announced last month were a good start but if that's where it ends then we are left far short of a credible fiscal consolidation.

Second, the FDI liberalisation steps were significant pro-reform, pro-investment signals. But for those signals to translate into a substantial and sustainable improvement in the climate for real investment (as distinct from reversible stock market plays), a good deal more needs to happen—especially against the background of the past few years of stalled projects, regulatory and scam-related bottlenecks in key sectors and widespread indications of slowing investment. There is no substitute for tackling the policy and regulatory constraints and uncertainties (especially relating to environment, land acquisition and fuel supply) in critical sectors such as power, coal, mining, roads, railways and telecom. For this to happen, a politico-administrative system rendered deeply defensive and dilatory by weak governance, scams and their aftermaths of the last few years has to be re-energised and redirected. A tall order under the best of circumstances. So it may be unrealistic to expect a quick rebound in real investment and growth.

Third, the recent surge in capital inflows is being mishandled. Instead of allowing the brunt of the inflows to be borne by an appreciating rupee, a good part of these inflows should be purchased by the Reserve Bank of India (RBI) to rebuild reserves. This would moderate the appreciation of the currency (and associated loss of competitiveness) and avoid the policy errors committed in 2009-10 when the real effective exchange of the rupee was allowed to rise steeply, to the subsequent detriment of our external deficits. Our CAD (current account deficit) remains exceptionally high at nearly 4 per cent of GDP and output and employment in manufacturing is stagnant. This is surely not the time to permit any significant nominal and real appreciation of the rupee.

Fourth, last week's cabinet approval of a slew of (mainly) financial sector related bills was a welcome sign of an awakened government. Several of the bills are hardy perennials which have been through the committee process in Parliament. But it is one thing to confer cabinet approval to a bill; quite another to pass it in Parliament. The insurance and pension amending bills will depend crucially on support from the Bharatiya Janata Party (BJP) when they are placed in Parliament in the winter session. So nothing is guaranteed. As for the proposed amendments to the Competition Act, the extension of the Commission's jurisdiction to mergers and acquisition of banks seems ill-advised, when these are already scrutinised by the specialist regulator, the RBI.

In sum, the measures taken so far are very welcome, even though long overdue. They have certainly had significant positive effects on portfolio capital inflows and market expectations. It is too early to assess their effect on real investment and output. The combined fiscal deficit for this year is still slated to be too high at close to 8 per cent of GDP and the government's commitment to a medium-term fiscal consolidation programme remains to be announced.

The external trade and current account deficits also remain close to record highs and apprehensions of external vulnerability are hardly assuaged by the authorities' willingness to allow significant nominal and real appreciation of the rupee. Until the bottlenecks and policy uncertainties in key infrastructure sectors are tackled seriously, the chances of an appreciable positive turnaround in growth, employment and inflation prospects remain small. The associated stresses on the financial sector continue to be uncomfortably high.

In a way, the measures announced over the past month have put the brakes on the prolonged downhill slide in macroeconomic performance. But by themselves they are probably insufficient to bring about a significant and sustainable reversal in the negative trends in growth, fiscal deficits, external imbalances, inflation and employment. For that, we need stronger and sustained policy actions for fiscal consolidation, infrastructure performance and real reform. Until then, economic growth is likely to hover in the range of 5-7 per cent, perhaps even 5-6 per cent. The flashing lights are still amber.

----

11 October 2012.

10

Fiscal Consolidation: How Real?

On 29 October 2012, the Finance Minister issued a statement laying out the government's roadmap for fiscal consolidation during the period of the Twelfth Five Year Plan, 2012/13-2016/17. Specifically, he committed that the fiscal deficit of the central government would be held at 5.3 per cent of GDP (gross domestic product) in 2012-13 and then reduced gradually to 4.8 per cent in 2013-2014, 4.2 per cent in 2014-15, 3.6 per cent in 2015-16 and, finally, 3.0 per cent in 2016-17. Amongst that tiny fraction of India's population interested in such matters, there has been much ennui and cynicism expressed about this roadmap. After all, they have seen many such fiscal plans announced and then ignored over the last few years. Recall that the 13th Finance Commission laid out a roadmap three years back, which envisaged the central government deficit being reduced to 3 per cent of GDP by 2013-14! In the three budgets presented since then by Mr Pranab Mukherjee, the Commission's recommended trajectory was brushed aside and replaced by successive and increasingly weaker consolidation paths outlined in the accompanying, 3-year Medium Term Fiscal Policy Statements, inconveniently required by the fiscal responsibility law. Basically, these statements simply kept postponing the real fiscal consolidation required.

Nevertheless, I would suggest that Mr Chidambaram's new roadmap for consolidation has to be taken seriously and evaluated accordingly. It comes at a time when the country's economic situation has worsened seriously on every front: growth, inflation, external deficits and vulnerability, infrastructure bottlenecks and even governance. Aside from many warnings by independent analysts (this author included) over the past three years, this September's Kelkar Committee report paints an authoritative and grim picture. In his statement, last week, Mr Chidambaram rightly emphasises the centrality of fiscal corrections to deal with the very difficult macroeconomic situation: "As fiscal consolidation takes place and investors' confidence increases, it is expected that the economy will return to the path of high investment, higher growth and long term sustainability".

Before turning to evaluate the realism of the new roadmap, it is pertinent to highlight one little-remarked perspective on the trajectory of fiscal deficits in India. At least for the last decade, we have two different official series, one published by the Reserve Bank of India (RBI) in its various publications and the other by the Prime Minister's Economic Advisory Council (PMEAC). The numbers are pretty much the same except for the four years, 2005-06 to 2008-09 (see Table 10.1). In each of those four years, and especially in 2008-09, the fiscal deficit of the centre, as well as the combined one (centre and states), cited by PMEAC is significantly higher than that shown by the RBI. The difference is that PMEAC includes the substantial recourse to 'off-budget liabilities', mainly in the form of petroleum and fertiliser bonds, that was resorted to by the finance ministry (headed by the present minister), whereas the RBI series omits them. As I have pointed out elsewhere ("Oil Bonds are No Solution", *Business Standard*, 22 May 2008), PMEAC's more inclusive definition is better both for assessing the economic consequences of fiscal deficits and for keeping track of government debt.

The reason for digging up this recent history is that for fiscal consolidation to have the expected desirable consequences in terms of reduced inflation, higher savings and investment, higher growth and lower external deficits, the consolidation has to be real and not a product of clever accounting practices. So we must hope that the current roadmap is referring to 'real' fiscal deficits.

How realistic is the present road map? Let's start with the current year, 2012-13. As compared to the 5.1 per cent of GDP target in Mr Pranab Mukherjee's March budget, the September report of the Kelkar Committee foresaw a deficit of 6.1 per cent of GDP on a 'business as usual' scenario, entailing grave and unacceptable consequences for the economy. It went on to recommend a slew of corrective measures including: increases in the prices of controlled petroleum products, fertiliser and foodgrain distributed from public stocks; full decontrol of sugar; a new system for accelerated disinvestment; postponement of the Food Security Bill; a detailed array of tax measures to raise the fallen tax-to-GDP ratio; and a substantial cut in Plan expenditures. The mid-September price increases in diesel and LPG (liquified petroleum gas) cylinders may reduce the fiscal deficit by 0.2 per cent of GDP. Mr Chidambaram's recent roadmap commends some of the Kelkar recommendations, with the notable exceptions of price increases in food and fertiliser and sugar decontrol. Nor is there any mention of further increases in petroleum products or postponement of the Food Security Bill. The statement does express confidence in meeting the budget targets for disinvestment and 'non-tax receipts' (including ₹40,000 crore of telecom 2G spectrum auction proceeds).

Consider the following facts. First, by end September, the government's tax receipts amounted to less than 40.0 per cent of the year's budget target. Second, to date not one rupee of the ₹30,000 crore disinvestment target has been realised. Third, detailed analyses in the 30 October and 6 November issues of this paper suggest that spectrum auction receipts may fall short by as much as 50 per cent of the anticipated ₹40,000 crore. Fourth, the political likelihood of price increases in fertiliser and food and sugar decontrol looks pretty low. Fifth, there seems to be some back-pedalling in implementing the LPG cylinder cap scheme announced in September. Against this background, it is hard to see how the fiscal deficit can be significantly lower than the 6.1 per cent estimated by the Kelkar Committee. A reasonable guess might be around 5.8 or 5.9 per cent of GDP, well above the 5.3 per cent stated in the minister's roadmap. This, of course, assumes the absence of novel accounting practices of the petro-bond kind.

Quite apart from the additional borrowing that the government will have to undertake (perhaps ₹60,000-₹80,000 crore more than the budget estimate) and its negative consequences, the real problem is that such an outcome will indicate a total failure of fiscal consolidation in 2012-13. Furthermore, if this happens, it will make the deficit targets for subsequent years, especially the pre-election year of 2013-2014, look seriously infeasible. None of this should be surprising, given the gigantic jump in government spending in 2008-09 in the form of pay increases, subsidies and entitlement programme expansions. Stimuli they certainly were, but not of an easily reversible kind! So, despite all earnest government statements to the contrary, 2012-2013 may well see a combined fiscal deficit of around 8.0 per cent of GDP...just like 2011-12. And may be 2013-14 as well? In the absence of fiscal correction, we should lower our hopes for an early revival of investment and growth.

Table 10.1

Two Official Estimates of Fiscal Deficits (% of GDP)

Year	Central Government		Combined (Central plus State Governments)	
	(1)	(2)	(3)	(4)
	PMEAC [1]	*RBI* [2]	*PMEAC* [1]	*RBI* [2]
2002-03	6.0	5.9	9.7	9.6
2003-04	4.6	4.5	8.7	8.5
2004-05	3.9	3.9	7.3	7.2
2005-06	4.7	4.0	7.3	6.5
2006-07	4.3	3.3	6.3	5.4
2007-08	3.1	2.5	4.7	4.0
2008-09	8.2	6.0	10.6	8.3
2009-10	6.6	6.5	9.4	9.4
2010-11	4.9	4.9	6.9	6.9
2011-12 (RE)	5.9	5.9	8.2	8.2
2012-13 (BE)	5.1	5.1	7.1	7.1

Note: 1_/: Prime Minister's Economic Advisory Council (PMEAC), *Economic Outlook 2012-13*, August 2012. Includes off-budget liabilities.

2_/: Reserve Bank of India (RBI), *Handbook of Statistics on the Indian Economy, 2011-12* and *Annual Report, 2011–12*.

09 November 2012.

11

India's Economic Growth
Trends and Imbalances

Most people are familiar with the trajectory of India's economic growth in the last 20 years, since the external payments crisis of 1991. Just to briefly refresh memories, following three decades of growth at below 4.0 per cent a year between 1950 and 1980 and the modest acceleration to 5.4 per cent in the 1980s, the external payments crisis of 1991 triggered wide-ranging economic reforms, which in turn raised the GDP (gross domestic product) growth rate to 6.6 per cent in the five years, 1992-1997. Then came the East Asian crisis, a succession of poor harvests, a couple years of fractious coalition governance and renewed fiscal profligacy, which combined to drag down the economy's growth to the pre-reforms average of 5.4 per cent in the six years, 1997-2003. Fortunately, under National Democratic Alliance (NDA) governments of 1998-2004, economic reforms revived and, together with the ensuing global economic boom, laid the basis for the exceptional surge in economic growth in 2003-2008, averaging almost 9.0 per cent a year. In the next four years, 2009-2012, India weathered the initial down-draft from the global economic crisis quite well, only to be tripped up by mounting deficiencies in domestic economic policies, which saw growth drop to 6.5 per cent in 2011-12 and below 6.0 per cent in the current year. Thanks to the initial resilience, average growth for the four years, 2009-2012, came to 7.5 per cent, which now looks quite enviable, from the perspective result of 5.5 per cent from the first half 2012-13.

The point of this column is not to rehash this well-trodden ground. Rather, the purpose is to look at some of the broad trends in the composition of growth (by major sectors and expenditure components) embedded in the national accounts data of the past two decades, and to highlight a few key points. The last 20 years have been partitioned into four sub-periods: the initial, reforms-fuelled growth surge of 1992-1997; the next six years of moderate growth in 1997-2003; the remarkable five-year boom of 2003-2008; and the most recent four years of deceleration in 2008-2012.

Let us begin with the sectoral growth patterns in the upper panel of the table. Inspection reveals some noteworthy trends:

- First, the reforms-led growth burst of 1992-1997 was remarkably well balanced, with agriculture contributing a fifth of the total growth, industry (excluding construction) over a quarter and services (including construction) just over half.

- Second, industry was particularly dynamic, contributing well over its early nineties share of 20 per cent in GDP.

- Third, the next three sub-periods are much less 'balanced', with the services sector accounting for the predominant share in GDP growth, amounting to as much as 80 per cent in the periods 1997-2003 and 2008-2012, and almost 70 per cent in the exceptional growth boom of 2003-2008.

- Fourth, agriculture contributed little in these three sub-periods and, as a result, saw its share of GDP halve from nearly 30 per cent in the early 1990s to less than 15 per cent in 2009-2012.

- Fifth, while the contribution of industry to GDP growth fluctuated (and never again attained the level achieved in 1992-1997), the share of industry in GDP remained fairly static at 20 per cent throughout.

- Sixth, this meant that the entire drop of 15 per cent in the share of agriculture in GDP 'accrued' to services, whose share rose steeply from 51 per cent in the early 1990s to 66 per cent in 2009-2012.

This dominantly services-led growth pattern is certainly better than an alternative of more sectorally balanced but slower growth. However, as I have pointed out elsewhere (*Business Standard*, 23 December 2003), it does raise issues of sustainability for the long run. It is also surely worrisome to see the prolonged stagnation in the share of industry, of which four-fifth is accounted for by India's stunted manufacturing sector. Of related and perhaps greater concern is the slow change in the sectoral composition of India's labour force: although agriculture's share in GDP has dropped below 15.0 per cent, the sector's share in total employment remains worryingly high at 50.0 per cent or so. This is essentially because of slow growth of employment in services and industry (see my article in *Business Standard*, 10 December 2009).

Let us now turn to the demand or expenditure side of the story for some noteworthy points (see lower panel of the table):

- The big story here is the role of investment demand (fixed and other), especially during the boom of 2003-2008, when it surged to account for 64.0 per cent of the increase in aggregate expenditure. Even during the less dynamic periods of 1997-2003 and 2008-2012, investment demand contributed 35.0 per cent. These increases raised the share of aggregate investment from 23.0 per cent in GDP in the early 1990s to 38.0 per cent in 2009-2012.

- On the other hand, the decline in the relative contribution of investment, especially fixed investment, in the most recent years of 2008-2012 is a cause for serious concern. The rising share of investment in stocks and valuables (notably gold) in GDP in recent years is also a mixed blessing, as much of it reflects excess food stocks and additions to gold hoards.

- Third, private consumption demand has contributed less than its GDP share in all periods to propelling growth. As a result, the share of private consumption in GDP has fallen from 66.0 per cent in the early 1990s to 58.0 per cent in 2009-2012.

- Fourth, the other component of demand which has fallen, to make room for the rise in the share of investment in GDP, is net exports of goods and services, that is, exports minus imports. This has gone from -0.9 per cent of GDP in 1990-1993 to -6.7 per cent in 2009-2012, and is reflected in the sharp increase in the CAD (current account deficit) in the balance of payments in the last three years.

- Fifth, the contribution of government consumption to aggregate expenditure growth has waxed and waned, typically falling during periods of fiscal consolidation and rising during those of fiscal profligacy. It is surely no comfort that the most recent period of 2008-2012 has been one of the renewed fiscal excess, especially given that such periods have coincided with times of lower economic growth.

To achieve more balanced and faster economic growth in future, investment, exports and industry have to grow much faster than they have in recent years.

Table 11.1

Sectoral and Expenditure Contributions to Growth and Shares in GDP

	Contributions to Growth (% share)				Sectoral Shares (% of GDP)		
	1992-1997	1997-2003	2003-2008	2008-2012	1990-1993	2000-2003	2009-2012
Average GDP Growth (%)	6.6	5.4	8.7	7.5			
By Sectors							
Agriculture	19.9	3.8	10.3	5.6	29.1	21.6	14.4
Industry	26.4	17.0	20.7	15.0	20.2	20.4	19.8
Services	53.3	79.9	68.7	79.6	50.7	57.9	65.8
By Expenditure Components					*Expenditure Shares (% of GDP)*		
Private Consumption	53.0	55.6	51.2	57.3	66.0	63.6	57.9
Government Consumption	8.5	13.9	7.3	14.0	12.0	12.7	11.2
Gross Fixed Investment	25.0	29.1	51.3	26.9	22.2	24.9	32.1
Investment in Stocks and Valuables	-3.8	5.8	12.8	8.1	0.7	1.1	5.5
Net Exports of Goods and Services	-7.7	0.7	-10.6	-16.1	-0.9	-2.2	-6.7

Note: The "Contributions to Growth" may not sum up to 100 per cent, especially in respect of expenditure components because of substantial 'discrepancies' in the data.

Source: Reserve Bank of India, *Handbook of Statistics on the Indian Economy, 2011-12.*

---

10 January 2013.

12

Macroeconomic Context and Budget

A bit like a broken gramophone record (if anybody remembers those shiny black 78s, 45s and 33s which enriched our youth), I have been bemoaning the grievous deterioration in India's macroeconomic performance, and its underlying causes, in various articles over the past two years. These grim warnings and many similar commentaries by other analysts have had little impact on either the curious combination of complacence and helplessness of the government or on the seemingly inexorable downward spiral of the economy. Last week's publication by the Central Statistical Organisation (CSO) of the Advance Estimates for National Income for 2012-13 drove home just how bad the situation has become. Real GDP (gross domestic product) at factor cost is estimated to have grown by just 5.0 per cent, as compared to 9.3 per cent in 2010-11. GDP growth in market prices was even lower, a mere 3.3 per cent, darkly reminiscent of the so-called 'Hindu rate of growth' of our pre-1980 decades.

The finance ministry promptly (and most unusually) issued official statements that the CSO had got it wrong; growth would be 5.5 per cent, not 5.0. This pointless squabble over half a percentage point came from a ministry which predicted 9.0 per cent growth (at budget time) for 2011-12, when the result has been 6.2 per cent and last March predicted 7.5 per cent for 2012-13, when the result appears to be 5.0 per cent. For the mighty Finance Ministry, entrusted with the nation's macroeconomic management, to get its short-term growth projection wrong by 2.5-3.0 percentage points in two successive years is a new and deeply disturbing record...to put it mildly.

Sharply slowing economic growth is just one, albeit crucially important, facet of our bad economic performance since 2008. As the upper panel of the table reminds, our macro performance has worsened on every other major dimension as well, especially when compared to the 'golden age' of 2003-2008. Inflation, as measured by the broad-based GDP deflator has been unrelentingly high, at above 8.0 per cent in most years. This is in large part due to the prolonged fiscal profligacy of last five years: the combined (centre plus states) fiscal deficit more than doubled in 2008-09 from its post-consolidation low of 4.1 of GDP in 2007-08 and has stayed above 8.0 per cent of GDP ever since, except for a short-lived dip in 2010-11 because of massive receipts from one-off telecom spectrum sales. The BoP (balance of payments) has deteriorated steadily and ominously, with the current account deficit (or CAD in Wodehouse terminology) increasing from less than half a per cent of GDP in 2003-2008 to nearly 3.0 per cent in 2009-10 and 2010-11, and worsening to record levels in excess of 4.0 per cent of GDP in 2011-12 and 2012-13. In part, this reflects the substantial decline in gross domestic savings from 37.0 per cent of GDP in 2007-08 to around 30.0 per cent at present. The main culprits have been government savings and corporate savings. Gross investment rates have also fallen, but by much less than savings. Indeed, the resilience of aggregate investment rates shown by the national accounts is hard to reconcile with all the other indicators of lacklustre investment such as weak capital goods production, stalled projects and slim order books. Perhaps worse news lies ahead?

It is against this increasingly grim macroeconomic scenario that the budget for 2013-14 is being framed. Fortunately, there is growing recognition that a reversal of the prolonged fiscal profligacy would help all the major macro problems by reducing inflationary pressures, easing the external imbalance and making room for more of productive investment. Hence, the finance minister's oft-repeated commitment to hold the central government's fiscal deficit for 2012-13 at 5.3 per cent of GDP and reduce it to 4.8 per cent in 2013-14 is very welcome. But how is this going to be done? Let us seek clues in recent fiscal trends, shown in the table's lower panel.

A quick inspection reveals some salient features of trends since the 'golden age' until 2011-12 (outcomes for 2012-13 are still unknown). Between 2007-08 and 2011-12, both fiscal and revenue deficits deteriorated by 3.5 per cent of GDP. About two-third of this worsening was due to declines in the ratio (to GDP) of revenue receipts, especially tax receipts (net of transfers to states). The total expenditure ratio also increased, but only modestly, because the rise in the revenue expenditure share by 1.2 per cent of GDP (mostly because of ballooning subsidies) was partially offset by a regrettable decline in the capital expenditure ratio by 0.6 per cent. Available data for 2012-13 suggest that these trends (in ratio terms) of falling revenues, rising revenue expenditures (especially subsidies) and declining capital expenditure have persisted through 2012-13. The recent increases in diesel prices will have limited effect in the current year. Reports of final quarter slashing of expenditures in defence and rural expenditures are unlikely to reverse these broad trends.

Against this background, to attain the pre-announced fiscal deficit target of 4.8 per cent of GDP in 2013-14, the forthcoming budget will have to keep a tight rein on expenditures, especially subsidies. The 'creeping liberalisation' of diesel prices will have to be adhered to. Something serious needs to be done to check the growth of fertiliser subsidies. Above all, the ill-designed Food Security Bill, will have to be kept at bay. Else even limited fiscal correction will remain a chimera. On the other side of the ledger, the budget will have to introduce measures to increase tax revenues. The guiding principle should be 'do no harm', unlike the disastrous budget for 2012-13. With industry reeling from the past years' regulatory and fiscal shocks, it would be best to leave the corporate tax rates alone. There is certainly scope for raising the personal income tax rate for the income bracket above ₹15 (or 20) lakh a year by around 3.0-5.0 percentage points. It might be better to do this through a surcharge, simply to maintain the 16-year-old stability in the 10.0-20.0-30.0 per cent basic rate structure. On the indirect taxes side, there is much room for increasing numerous concessional rates in excise. It would also help the movement towards uniform rates in the context of the forthcoming (hopefully soon) national GST (goods and services tax). Whether the general rate for Services and CENVAT (central value added tax) should be revised upwards by a per cent point or two from the current 12.0 per cent rate depends crucially on the planned structure of the GST.

All this should help engender the 4.8 per cent of GDP fiscal deficit target. This will improve macroeconomic conditions. But will it be enough to reignite investment and growth, significantly check inflation and reduce the burgeoning CAD? My guess is that it will help moderate inflation and begin the process of growth recovery. But because the damage inflicted in past years has been very heavy, recovery will be slow, leading to less than 6 per cent growth in 2013-14. The big unresolved macro worry is the record high CAD. There is little that this budget can do to solve that major vulnerability in a hurry.

14 February 2013.

Table 12.1

Macroeconomic and Fiscal Indicators

	2003/04-2007/08	2007/08	2008/09	2009/10	2010/11	2011/12	2012/13
Macroeconomic Indicators							
Economic Growth (GDP, % per year)	8.7	9.3	6.7	8.6	9.3	6.2	5.0
Inflation (GDP deflator, % per year)	5.6	6.6	8.8	7.5	10.5	8.7	8.2
Current Account Balance (% of GDP)	-0.3	-1.3	-2.3	-2.8	-2.7	-4.2	-4.5 *
Combined Fiscal Deficit (% of GDP)	6.3	4.1	8.5	9.5	7.0	8.2	8.0 *
Gross Domestic Investment (% of GDP)	33.8	38.1	34.3	36.6	36.8	35.0	34.0 *
Gross Fixed Investment (% of GDP)	29.6	32.9	32.3	31.6	31.7	30.6	29.9
Gross Domestic Savings (% of GDP)	33.4	36.8	32.0	33.8	34.0	30.8	29.5 *
Central Government Fiscal Indicators (As % of GDP)							
Total Revenue Receipts	9.9	10.9	9.6	8.9	10.3	8.7	
a) Tax Revenue (net)	7.6	8.8	7.9	7.1	7.4	7.3	
b) Non-tax Revenue	2.3	2.1	1.7	1.8	2.9	1.4	
Total Expenditure	14.8	14.3	15.7	15.9	15.6	14.9	
a) Revenue Expenditure	12.2	11.9	14.1	14.1	13.6	13.1	
of which: Subsidies	(1.4)	(1.4)	(2.3)	(2.2)	(2.3)	(2.4)	
b) Capital Expenditure	2.6	2.4	1.6	1.7	2.0	1.8	
Revenue Deficit	2.3	1.1	4.5	5.2	3.3	4.5	
Gross Fiscal Deficit	3.6	2.5	6.0	6.5	4.9	5.9	
Primary Deficit	-0.2	-0.9	2.6	3.2	1.8	2.8	

Note: * denotes author's projections.
Sources: CSO and Reserve Bank of India.

13

BoP: Zero Dark Thirteen

Fourteen months ago (Chapter 2) I warned that at least four crises were in the making: an external payments crisis, a crisis of several years of slow growth, a job scarcity crisis for the 'youth bulge' and a serious weakening of our national security capacity. Where do we stand today? Well, we seem to be well into the crisis of prolonged low growth: 6.2 per cent in 2011-12, 5.0 per cent this year and less than 6.0 per cent in 2013-14. Even if you take the government's more optimistic forecast for 2013-14, in the three years, 2012-13 to 2013-14, the Indian economy will have grown at less than 6.0 per cent a year—well below the risible Planning Commission expectations of 9.0 per cent plus hardly a year back. There are plenty of indications that the crisis of job scarcity for the burgeoning young population is also upon us, although we lack reliable, national data on the employment situation after 2009-10. Despite mounting threats to our national security, the budget allocations for our defence forces have been falling in recent years as a proportion of GDP (gross domestic product), testifying to the weakening of our defence capabilities.

Here my focus is on the first of the four crises mentioned above, namely the growing fragility of our external finances. The basic data in the table and graph are clear enough. Since 2003-04, our merchandise trade deficit has risen five-fold from 2.0 per cent of GDP to about 11.0 per cent at present. The CAD (current account deficit) has worsened in tandem, and is now running at a completely unsustainable 5.0 per cent of GDP, four times higher than the 1.0-1.3 per cent level of 2005-2008 and double the 2.5 per cent level indicated as sustainable and 'safe' by the Prime Minister and his senior economic colleagues, including in recent budget interviews. Basically, since 2005-2008, the trade deficit has widened by about 4.0 per cent of GDP, while the surplus on 'invisibles' (mostly software exports and remittances) has hardly risen as a share of GDP. As a result, the CAD has been higher than the safety benchmark of 2.5 per cent of GDP in each of the four years since 2009-10, and over 4 per cent in the two most recent years.

So, and this is important, our current external fragility has not appeared suddenly; it is a result of sustained neglect and economic mismanagement. Several strands of mismanagement can be readily identified (and have been, repeatedly, in these columns over the years). First, the high fiscal and revenue deficits of the last five years have spilled into the external sector, just as they did in the late 1980s. Second, the relatively hands-off approach to exchange rate management, adopted by the Reserve Bank of India (RBI) since spring 2009, has allowed a completely unjustifiable nominal and real appreciation of the rupee, especially in 2009-10, contributing to the burgeoning trade and current account deficits. This loss of external competitiveness has been exacerbated by the more recent policy disarray in core infrastructure and mining sectors, which has seriously hurt the manufacturing sector, and directly damaged exports and import-substituting, domestic production in mining. The problems have been further compounded by growing labour market inflexibilities and rising costs.

Of course, these policy failures have been magnified by some external factors, such as recessions in industrial nations and (somewhat paradoxically) high prices of oil and metals. But these are outside India's control; it does not absolve our policymakers from adjusting policies to deal with external problems. Instead, their approach seems to have neglected the difficult, 'bullet-biting' decisions and has preferred the soft option of seeking higher external financing (notably foreign direct and portfolio investment and external commercial borrowing) to plug the rising external deficits. The problem is that such financing has a proven track record of becoming scarce just when you need it most, especially when tax and regulatory policies are negative and unstable.

Does the recent budget significantly reduce our dangerously high external vulnerability? Not much. Consider the following. We need to reduce the gaping CAD fairly quickly, from around 5.0 per cent of GDP to 2.5 per cent. It is an accounting truism that this needs an equivalent reduction in the domestic savings-investment gap. Presumably, we would prefer that most of this comes from an increase in domestic savings rather than a further decrease in investment. One source is the central government budget. But this only targets a reduction in government dissavings (the revenue deficit) of 0.6 per cent of GDP from 3.9 per cent in 2012-13 to 3.3 per cent of GDP in 2013-14 (still thrice the level of 2007-08!); that is, only about one-fifth of the required reduction in the investment-savings gap. And that is if you believe the patently optimistic projections for tax revenues, spectrum auction receipts, disinvestment and subsidies! India's external vulnerability remains largely untended. We may still need $90 to $100 billion of net external financing in 2013-14.

How might vulnerability transform into crisis? It is, unfortunately, quite easy to envision plausible scenarios. For example, a return to 'risk off' in global markets could easily lead to a $10-20 billion reduction in foreign inflows in a short time period, triggering a rupee depreciation, which could become unmanageable as speculative leads and lags in current and capital account transactions swell in response. Sharp and disorderly currency depreciation would fuel inflation, seriously damage externally leveraged companies, weaken the banks exposed to such companies and generally disrupt economic activity. A similar scenario could be induced by a spike in oil prices. Indeed, even the publication of unexpectedly large trade and current account deficit results could trigger a damaging run on the rupee. When vulnerability is high, fairly modest external or internal economic shocks can precipitate a large problem.

What can be done? The hard truth is that there is no easy way to quickly reduce vulnerability, when policymakers have allowed the situation to deteriorate for so many years despite all the warning signals. The opportunities to resist rupee appreciation (in a context of growing deficits) and build-up forex reserves were missed earlier and may not return soon. The manifold costs of high fiscal deficits for five years cannot be rectified in a few months. Exports cannot be ramped up overnight when labour-intensive manufacturing has been penalised for many years by bad policies. What can be done is limited. It includes undertaking a sharper reduction in the revenue deficit than the budget has presented. The disarray in core sectors has to be addressed urgently. Forex reserves need to be deployed with finesse in the face of currency volatility. And, perhaps, the finance ministry should engage the International Monetary Fund (IMF) in discreet but serious discussions about emergency loan facilities, in case the liquidity crisis does hit.

None of this is palatable. But we need to remember that if the crisis does strike, it may be a lot harder to bounce back than in 1991. The global economic environment is much weaker. More importantly, the low-hanging fruits of easy policy reform were consumed earlier. Now the going will be much tougher. Meanwhile we have to hope for the best. We are good at that!

Figure 13.1

Rising External Deficits as Percentage of GDP

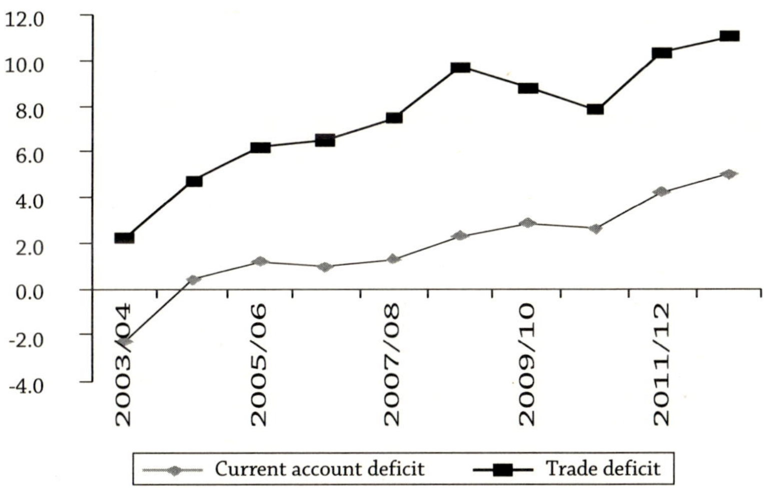

---

14 March 2013.

Table 13.1

Key Components of India's Balance of Payments (% of GDP)

No.	Component	2003-04	2004-05	2005-06	2006-07	2007-08	2008-09	2009-10	2010-11	2011-12	2012-13
1	Trade balance (A–B)	–2.2	–4.7	–6.2	–6.5	–7.4	–9.7	–8.7	–7.8	–10.3	-11.0
	A) Merchandise exports	10.7	11.8	12.6	13.6	13.4	15.2	13.4	14.8	16.8	
	B) Merchandise imports	13.0	16.5	18.8	20.1	20.8	25.0	22.0	22.6	27.1	
2	Invisibles, net	4.5	4.3	5.0	5.5	6.1	7.5	5.9	5.1	6.1	6.0
	Of which:										
	A) Software exports	2.0	2.3	2.7	3.3	3.2	3.8	3.6	3.5	3.3	
	B) Private transfers	3.5	2.8	2.9	3.1	3.4	3.6	3.8	3.2	3.4	
3	Current account balance	2.3	–0.4	–1.2	–1.0	–1.3	–2.3	–2.8	–2.6	–4.2	-5.0
4	Net capital inflows	2.8	4.0	3.0	4.8	8.7	0.5	3.8	3.4	3.6	5.0
	Of which:										
	A) Foreign direct investment	0.7	0.8	1.1	2.4	2.8	1.6	1.7	0.5	1.2	
	B) Foreign portfolio investment	1.8	1.3	1.5	0.7	2.2	–1.1	2.4	1.9	1.0	
	C) External assistance, net	–0.5	0.3	0.2	0.2	0.2	0.2	0.2	0.3	0.1	
	D) Commercial borrowings, net	–0.5	0.7	0.3	1.7	1.8	0.6	0.2	0.7	0.5	
5	Overall balance	5.1	3.6	1.8	3.8	7.4	–1.7	1.0	0.8	–0.8	0.0

Note: * Author's projections.
Sources: Reserve Bank of India.

14

Don't Blame the World

Over the past two or three years, as India's economic performance has deteriorated badly, it has become commonplace to hear senior members of government attribute most, if not all, of the worsening in economic performance to external factors. Typically, these have included the slow and uncertain recoveries from the global financial crisis in the US and Japan and the lingering crisis and recession in Europe. Let me agree straightaway that these are very real problems which have beset the global economy in recent years. Let me also agree that implications of these global frailties have been clearly negative for India's development potential. Where I part company with government spokesmen is in the relative weight attached to external and domestic factors in explaining India's weakened performance, especially in regard to the sharp slowdown in economic growth and the ratcheting up of external deficits.

Thus, and speaking heuristically, if government apologists assign perhaps 70.0 per cent plus of the country's poor economic performance to external causes and the remainder to domestic policy problems, I think it might be more accurate to reverse these relative weights, with domestic policy weaknesses shouldering most of the blame. To give an example, if the potential growth rate of the Indian economy was 9.0-10.0 per cent in the pre-global-crisis world, it may now be down to 7.0-8.0 per cent because of the weak global environment. But that surely does not explain the collapse of GDP (gross domestic Product) growth to barely 5.0 per cent. For that we have to invoke failures in domestic economic policy.

Aside from asserting a different point of view, what one can do to buttress one's case? One obvious answer is to look at the performance of other Asian developing countries like India. There is, of course, the difficulty of finding comparator nations 'like India'. A likely candidate is China, with its 1.35 billion inhabitants and significant developing country characteristics, despite her explosive growth in the last three and a half decades. A glance at the table shows that China's economic growth has also slowed in the last two years, but much less sharply than India's. Moreover, in the other three dimensions of macroeconomic performance, China has done rather well and far better than India. Inflation has been low (around 3.0-5.0%), compared to near double digits in India. A large part of the reason could be China's much stronger record in maintaining fiscal balance, with deficits running below 3.0 per cent of GDP, instead of the profligate 8.0-9.0 per cent of GDP level that has become the Indian norm after 2007-08.

Furthermore, despite having an economy much more open to international trade and capital flows than India and therefore potentially more vulnerable to global economic setbacks, China has managed to retain a comfortable surplus in its current account, running at 2.5-3.0 per cent of GDP in the last two years. And this is not because China's international trade has collapsed in the wake of the global crisis. In 2012, China's goods exports exceeded $2 trillion, nearly 70.0 per cent higher than in 2007 and almost seven times the level of India's 2012-13 exports!

Some will cavil, "you can't compare us to China; they are an $8 trillion economy, more developed than developing, and besides, they have a disciplined, authoritarian system of government, which makes them special." This counter carries little conviction in the present context of trying to identify the relative roles of external and domestic factors in explaining India's steep decline in economic performance. Never mind, let's move on to the next largest developing country in Asia, namely, Indonesia. With a population of 245 million, this nation is an order of magnitude less populous than India and China. On the other hand, in respect of socio-political system and stage of economic development Indonesia bears significant similarities to India. And the size of her economy is about half India's, not small by any means.

A notable feature of Indonesia's recent macroeconomic performance is the steadiness of her economic growth in the last three years, a little above 6.0 per cent in each year. There is no hint of a slowdown, despite her openness to foreign trade and capital flows being at least as much as India's. Inflation too has been moderate at around 5.0 per cent a year, a 'comfortable' level not seen in India during the last six years. Indonesia's moderate inflation levels may well be linked to her even more moderate fiscal deficits of less than 2.0 per cent of GDP in each of the last four years. The contrast with India's massive fiscal deficits is striking. Like China, Indonesia has also run surpluses on her external current account for most of the period, except for 2012. Taken together, the picture is one of responsible macroeconomic management, yielding good steady progress on the major indicators.

To sum up, our economic performance in the last three years has been markedly worse than that of China and Indonesia. Since all three countries engage with the same world economy, it is hard to make the case that global economic problems have hit India disproportionately hard. The much more plausible explanation for our unusually weak macroeconomic performance is surely the mismanagement of our own economic policies. Let us stop blaming the world.

Table 14.1

India, China and Indonesia : Recent Comparative Performance

GDP Growth (%)	2009	2010	2011	2012
India	8.6	9.3	6.2	5.0
China	9.2	10.4	9.3	7.8
Indonesia	4.6	6.2	6.5	6.2
Inflation (%)				
India	7.5	10.5	8.7	8.2
China	-0.7	3.3	5.4	2.6
Indonesia	4.8	5.1	5.4	4.3
Current Account Balance (% of GDP)				
India	-2.8	-2.7	-4.2	-5.0*
China	4.8	4.0	2.8	2.6
Indonesia	2.0	0.7	0.2	-2.8
Consolidated Fiscal Balance (% of GDP)				
India	-9.5	-7.0	-8.2	-8.0*
China	-2.2	-2.2	-1.3	-2.4
Indonesia	-1.6	-0.7	-1.1	-1.8

Notes: 1. For India, data are for fiscal years, thus, 2009 refers to 2009-10.; 2. Inflation relates to CPI for China and Indonesia and the GDP deflator for India; . "*" denotes author's projections.

Sources: CSO and RBI for India; IMF and Citibank for others.

---

11 April 2013.

15

Early Exit from Economic Stress?

As the government staggers from one corruption-related scandal to another, I am reminded of the title of an article I read some years ago, which characterised India as "a flailing state". The epithet seems increasingly appropriate. It certainly applies to the economic policies of recent years which have ensured the collapse of economic growth from 9.3 per cent in 2010-11 to 5.0 per cent in 2012-13, the yawning external imbalance with the CAD (current account deficit) officially expected to exceed 5 per cent of GDP in 2012-13 and consumer price inflation in double digits for the fourth successive year.

Faced by such ugly official data the government's response, from the Prime Minister down, has been to speak soothingly about the worst being behind us and predict a return to 8 per cent economic growth in three years, and a reduction of the CAD to 2.5 per cent of GDP in a similar period. For this year, 2013-14, the finance ministry projects (*via* the *Economic Survey, 2012-13*) a growth revival to 6.1-6.7 per cent, a prediction dutifully reflected by last fortnight's "Review of the Economy, 2012-13" by the Prime Minister's Economic Advisory Council (PMEAC), which foresees GDP (gross domestic product) growth of 6.4 per cent. The Reserve Bank of India (RBI), perhaps the most professional of extant official economic agencies, offered a more bearish forecast of 5.7 per cent in its *Monetary Policy Statement, 2013-14* last week.

What is one to make of all this? Will economic growth recover fairly soon as the finance ministry and PMEAC project? Or more slowly as forecast by the RBI? What will bring about the growth revival? Can the record high external imbalance (CAD) be halved within three years? What is the outlook for inflation? The search for answers must begin with a better understanding of what brought about the extraordinary deceleration of India's growth in the last two years. It wasn't the rate of aggregate investment in the economy, which remained at a surprisingly robust 35 per cent of GDP even in 2012-13. There was some worsening of the global economic environment but nothing comparable to the global crisis and recession of 2007-2009, which the Indian economy withstood remarkably well. Yes, some medium-term factors were at work, such as the prolonged absence of productivity-enhancing reforms and a slowing of services sector growth after many years of rapid expansion. But these do not explain the collapse of growth within two short years.

A more probable cause is the onset of major supply side constraints that have bedevilled the Indian economy since 2010, including: the sudden tightening of environmental regulations (including stalling of completed projects like the Lavasa township, the Mundra port in Gujarat and the Vedanta mining enterprise in Odisha); the eruption of serious scams in the Commonwealth Games, 2G telecom spectrum auction and coal block allocations and their debilitating aftermaths for the impacted sectors; the sweeping judicial restraints on iron ore mining in Karnataka and Goa; the fiasco of missing fuel supply (coal and gas) for many thousands of megawatts of newly completed power projects; and the generalised 'policy paralysis' and governance lacunae in regard to activation, completion and clearances of major core sector projects. In effect, these factors, taken together, dealt the Indian economy a serious (and still enduring) domestic supply shock in 2010-2012, which was majorly responsible for the collapse of economic growth in the last two years. As the PMEAC report puts it, "projects with large sums of money invested in them were not getting completed and therefore not yielding the expected current output".

If this broad diagnosis is accepted, then several implications follow for the appropriate sequencing of corrective policy. First, further loosening of monetary policy will not help significantly to restore growth. It will simply fuel inflation and inflationary expectations, which are still running in double digits (as the RBI's recent policy statement concedes), if one focuses on the broad CPI (consumer price index) as one should, now that we have one. In an economy with over 60 per cent of income generation and spending accounted for by services, the CPI is surely to be preferred to the WPI (wholesale price index), which omits services items. Reducing policy rates against the background of a record high CAD is also surely anomalous. Even if such reduction induced higher investment (highly unlikely in the present environment), that would simply aggravate the domestic savings-investment gap and the CAD. Lower policy rates would also damp the flow of financial savings which have dropped markedly in the last two years.

Second, more expansionary fiscal policy would also be counter-productive. For at least three of the last five years, our fiscal and revenue deficits have been running way too high, sustaining high levels of inflation, reducing government and domestic savings and exacerbating the massive external imbalance. As I have pointed (chapter 13), the recent government budget does little to reduce the CAD through higher government savings. What we need on the fiscal front is lower fiscal and revenue deficits and a shift in the composition of government expenditures away from subsidies and entitlement programmes and towards 'last mile' public investments.

Third, and above all, the first priority for policy must be to blunt the prevailing supply shock through administrative and coordination measures, which activate production from idled projects (fuel-starved power plants) and mines (iron ore and coal) and focus on completing major stalled projects in public and private sectors. The Cabinet Committee on Investment was established to secure this goal and the jury is still out on its effectiveness in the current fractious political climate. If the administrative/regulatory/judicial logjam can be loosened, there could be a quick yield in higher output, which would have multiplier constraint-loosening effects on the economy as well as lead to higher savings, a critical prerequisite for reducing the domestic savings-gap and thus help reduced the unsustainably high CAD.

That brings us back to India's short-term outlook for growth revival. What are the prospects for doing the right things effectively in the present environment of disappointingly weak governance, fiercely partisan politics and uncertain coordination across key economic agencies and ministries? Not too bright I would say. Add to that the available facts on the economy's trajectory. There is no significant evidence of the much-hoped-for turnaround or 'green shoots'. On the contrary, there are several signs that growth could slow further in the near term. So, with little optimism, we could hope for growth in the 5.0-6.0 per cent range in 2013-14. At this juncture, reverting to 8.0 per cent growth in three years looks like a distant mirage. And who knows whether even the 5.0-6.0 per cent can be sustained if our high external vulnerability is hit by shortages of foreign capital inflows.

09 May 2013.

16

Tightening Constraints to Rapid Inclusive Development

The current economic discussion focuses on managing the ongoing stresses on our external finances and an almost desperate search to revive economic growth from its meagre 5.0 per cent annual rate. As chapters 13 and 15 point out, neither of these is going to be easy. Let us lift our gaze beyond these short run exigencies and assess the prospects for reverting to a high (and inclusive) growth trajectory in the medium term. The outlook does not look too promising if one examines the array of unattended constraints that are getting sharper by the year. To keep it manageable, let me focus on just four such constraints, which have strong socio-political roots that render them especially intractable.

Anti-Employment Laws

Twenty years after a draft cabinet note was readied to loosen our exceptionally restrictive labour laws (one of Indira Gandhi's most damaging, anti-poor economic legacies), no progress has been achieved. The consequences continue to be profoundly (and increasingly) negative. Sixty-five years after Independence, over 90.0 per cent of our 500-million strong labour force eke out their living in 'informal sector' occupations with scant job security and low incomes. Industrial employers have every reason to avoid taking on new 'regular' employees and to shy away from large-scale operations in labour-intensive sectors like textiles, garments, leather products, toys and electronics, which were the hallmark of hugely successful employment-intensive industrialisation in East Asia since 1970. Little wonder that formal sector wage employment has stagnated, total employment has grown little in the most recent period (2004-

05 to 2009-10) for which reasonable data is available and the share of agriculture in total employment has remained unusually high (around 50.0%) despite the sharp drop in the sector's share in GDP (gross domestic product) (to 15.0%). The much-touted 'demographic dividend' of a youth bulge is being frittered away by our benighted labour policies and could easily morph into a massive, intractable problem of job scarcity, unemployment and underemployment.

The huge disincentives to employ workers in large and medium size industrial units has also seriously stunted the growth of our manufacturing sector, which has stagnated at 15.0-16.0 per cent of GDP for many years, compared to 30.0 per cent plus in most East Asian nations including China. Of course, other factors have also mattered but probably less than our exceptionally restrictive labour laws. With the stagnation of labour-intensive manufacturing, where will the 'youth bulge' find low-skill employment?

In sum, our labour laws continue to grievously weaken the most effective mechanism for assuring 'inclusiveness' in the development process for our most abundant resource of low-skill labour.

Fiscal Populism

Broadly defined, the second major constraint on rapid, broad-based growth is the penchant for fiscal populism, fuelled by competitive, short-horizon, politics at all levels of government. This has at least two dimensions: a propensity for premature launching of ill-designed entitlement programmes (for example, legal rights to work, education, food and so on); and a widespread 'subsidy culture'. The first has been massively strengthened during the last nine years of United Progressive Alliance (UPA) government, without first undertaking the reforms necessary to make these programmes effective and efficient. This means continuation of massive leakages (for example, estimated at 50.0 per cent and higher in the public food distribution system), rampant corruption and rent-seeking and strong vested interests against reform (to, say, conditional cash transfers or voucher systems). Both types of fiscal populism spawn high fiscal deficits with their attendant growth-retarding dangers of high inflation, large external imbalances and high interest rates and debt.

The second, 'the subsidy culture' has a longer history and continues to undermine the economic viability of key sectors. Electricity subsidies (especially for agriculture) have contributed majorly to the parlous situation of our electric power sector. They have also led to over-pumping and falling water tables in much of north and west India, amplifying the looming crisis in water availability. Foodgrain subsidies have distorted the agricultural economy and retarded the development of non-food crops. The growing subsidy on urea fertiliser has seriously weakened soil fertility. The massive diesel subsidy (now declining) has weakened energy security and hurt the environment. The explosive growth of mobile telephony in the last 15 years has demonstrated that subsidies are unnecessary for high growth and inclusive reach of a sector. But old habits die hard.

Weaknesses in Governance and Administration

Governance and administration are huge subjects. They clearly affect all dimensions of economic and social life, especially for poorer segments of society. They determine the quality of personal safety, justice, property rights, contract enforcement and the delivery of publicly provided goods and services. Worryingly, there are clear signs that governance has been deteriorating over time. There are at least two broad reasons for this. First, over time, politics has become more of a 'business' and less about public service and ideological commitment. Huge sums are raised and spent on campaigning for office and 'politicking' between elections (mostly under the table), which have then to be paid off by various subversions of public policies and decisions. 'Crony capitalism' has increased greatly, especially in resource sectors, such as mining, land allocation/use, telecom spectrum and large government contracts.

Secondly, it is generally agreed that the quality and probity of civil services has worsened over time for many reasons, including: the quality of entrants (for decades, many of the best people have opted for the growing opportunities outside government services); the ramping up of caste-based reservations or quotas since 1990, which has severely diluted the meritocracy principle; the increasing 'politicisation' of public administration at all levels; and the growing spread of bribery and corruption in government-citizen transactions. Taken together, the entropy in governance is likely to hurt future development.

The Challenge of Urbanisation

Normally, development experience worldwide suggests that urbanisation is associated with higher productivity and growth. However, in India, this association may be diluted by the well-known weakness of governance institutions in our cities and towns. Can anyone recall the name of a prominent mayor? Until the early 1990s the Indian Constitution did not recognise sub-national governments below the level of state governments. The 'third tier' was missing. The passage of the 73rd and 74th Amendments in 1993 corrected this lacuna and accorded a role to *panchayati raj* rural elected institutions and ULBs (urban local bodies). Although this was a major step forward, municipalities and other ULBs remain largely fledgling institutions with limited powers for mobilising and allocating resources.

Against this background, the expected increase in India's urban population by over 200 million between 2010 and 2030 poses a daunting challenge for urban governance. While there are some signs of hope, the general outlook is far from reassuring. Without a much more serious effort at urban institution building by the central and state governments, the realistic prospect is for rapid expansion of ill-governed and under-financed urban habitations, which impede reaping of the economies of agglomeration associated with well-functioning cities and towns. Such inchoate urbanisation may prove less an asset and more a drag on rapid, inclusive development in the long term.

So, all things considered, the return to high growth with inclusion poses arduous challenges in the years ahead.

13 June 2013.

II

Crisis

17

Shrinking India

Yes, the Gandhi-Singh government appears to have achieved this through its disappointingly bad economic and social policies. The toxic brew of fiscal populism, crony capitalism and bad economic management has ensured the collapse of economic growth, industrial stagnation, stubbornly high consumer inflation, declining savings and investment, shrinking employment opportunities, and a dangerously vulnerable external financing situation.

The current economic crisis has been building for several years. For a brief while, since last autumn, it looked as if the government had, at last, grasped the gravity of India's economic predicament and begun to take steps to turn things around. After many years of a reforms drought, a significant economic reform, the opening up of multi-brand retail to FDI (foreign direct investment) had been announced. At long last, the massive diesel subsidies had begun to be tackled through a stated policy of incremental price increases, while the LPG (liquefied petroleum gas) subsidies were sought to be contained through a dual-pricing mechanism. A fiscal consolidation path had been laid out, which the February 2013 budget manfully (if not entirely credibly) strove to approximate. A Cabinet Committee on Investment had been established to break the logjam in key infrastructure and industrial sectors, which had built up since 2010 in the wake of several high-profile scams and the resulting policy paralysis.

However, as the decline in the rupee's value since April has shown, it was probably a case of too little too late. This was particularly true of the government's management of external finances. After allowing the foreign trade deficit (in goods) to build inexorably from 6 per cent of GDP in 2005-06 to 11.0 per cent in 2012-13, and the CAD (current account deficit) to quintuple from 1.0 per cent of GDP to 5.0 per cent over the same period, the vulnerability to external and internal shocks and uncertainties could not be reduced in a hurry. Besides, the government's approach in the past year seems to have been focused on finding ways to finance the mounting CAD through more borrowing and investment inflows, rather than undertake the structural economic reforms necessary to reduce the CAD. Perhaps the underlying strategy was that the CAD could be somehow financed/managed until the next general elections, after which either a re-elected government could return to take the necessary tough measures or the mess would be dumped on the winning opposition combination.

Well, if that was the strategy, it isn't working too well. Against the US dollar, the rupee has depreciated by over 10 per cent in less than two months, despite the government's frantic efforts to raise more external financing and discourage gold imports and the Reserve Bank of India's (RBI) various measures to reduce 'speculation'. The basic problem is that India's external vulnerability is too high at a time when the medium-term outlook for global liquidity is getting bearish (QE [quantitative easing] tapering and all that) and capital flows to emerging nations are being reassessed. The chickens from the earlier 'borrow to finance CAD' approach are also coming home to roost. Even if the CAD comes down this year to $70-80 billion, over $170 billion of India's $390 billion external debt has to be paid off (or rolled over) during this year. These are all well-known, public facts, which suggest that the rupee will continue to be under downward pressure throughout the year and beyond. That, in itself, discourages new capital inflows and encourages exits by current holders of rupee assets. In this environment, the chances of staving off a deeper crisis until next May's general election don't look too good.

As if these pressures were not enough, the government may have blundered in going ahead with two retrograde policies in the last fortnight. First, as many have pointed out (including, Devesh Kapur in *Business Standard*, 8 July), the decision to enact the deeply flawed Food Security Bill through an ordinance promises higher fiscal deficits, more inflation, bigger distortions in agriculture and greater water stress. It confirms the worry that in the midst of a developing macroeconomic crisis, this government remains inexplicably committed to ill-designed, populist initiatives. Second, the announcement of the new gold-plated, gas-pricing formula (including for existing capacities!) strengthens concerns about the government's susceptibility to crony capitalism, and further erodes the financial viability of the hugely stressed electric power sector. When India's economic policies are under increasing external scrutiny, such policies could further discourage external capital inflows.

So what now? Sensible economic reforms are not in sight. In any case, if they require legislative approval, that is unlikely to be forthcoming. Nor are ordinances likely to be deployed to implement sensible reforms, since, almost by definition, they lack the appeal of populist measures. Making earlier announced measures work through the exercise of administrative will and capacity offers some hope. This might be true for making the FDI in retail initiative actually workable, something that has eluded the government for quite a few months. Even more important is the work of the Cabinet Committee on Investment in ensuring necessary approvals and clearances for stalled and 'shovel ready' projects. It is disheartening to note that the 29 June issue of the *London Economist* estimates (p.67) the "fresh capital investment" this committee has actually sanctioned in the six months, since its inception last December, amounts to only "0.4 per cent of GDP, spread over several years." If you are an incurable optimist, you could say that simply underlines the potential to do much more!

More realistically, we can expect external financing pressures to continue and perhaps worsen, while the economy continues to stutter. The recent bout of depreciation will, in time, discourage imports and encourage exports and import substitution. But that will take some time. What takes much less time is for the adverse impact on prices of imported goods and services, on the operating margins of import-dependent enterprises and on the debt service obligations of companies loaded with external loans. So inflation could tick upwards again and the fiscal deficit widens (higher subsidies for oil and fertiliser), while quite a few Indian companies feel the heat of the declining rupee. And that pain is likely to be transmitted back to the banks who have lent them money, at a time when the banking system (especially government-owned banks) are under significant stress already. So, the outlook for the rupee remains "volatile with a downward bias".

It's not a pretty picture. But then a stressed economy is rarely photogenic. The tragedy is that almost all of this was avoidable through better economic policy. It isn't rocket science. But it does require sustained wisdom, integrity and will in the political leadership. Otherwise, India shrinks.

11 July 2013.

18

A Crisis Foretold

Yes, we are in an economic crisis, albeit in its early stages. How else would you describe a situation where economic growth has collapsed, industrial output has stagnated for two years, jobs are being shed, consumer inflation is close to 10.0 per cent, the CAD (current account deficit) in the BoP (balance of payments) is nearly 5.0 per cent of GDP (gross domestic product) at last count, investment is fleeing abroad, external debt maturing in the current fiscal year exceeds $170 billion and the rupee is touching new lows (or highs against the $!) each week? It was all avoidable, if our policymakers had been more competent and effective (and less venal, some might add). There was plenty of warning commentary by independent analysts (this columnist included) over the past five years as each major policy misstep was taken. For the record and for future lesson-drawing, it is useful to briefly outline the five biggest economic policy mistakes (out of a long list), aside from the pervasive nine-year long drought of productivity-enhancing economic reforms.

Fiscal Blowout of 2008-09

In the six years to 2007-08, the combined (centre and states) fiscal deficit had been brought down from nearly 10.0 per cent of GDP to 4.0 per cent. This remarkable fiscal consolidation was squandered in the single, pre-election of year of 2008-09 when the combined deficit (inclusive of off-budget items) leapt to over 10.0 per cent of GDP. The central government budget deficit target of 2.5 per cent of GDP, presented by the current finance minister in February 2008, was massively overshot in the course of the year to yield an outcome of 8.2 per cent of GDP (including off-budget items), easily the biggest overshooting in India's history. Although later rationalised as 'fiscal stimulus' to counteract global crisis, in fact, the great bulk of the overshooting occurred before the Lehman crisis of September 2008, mainly in the form of pay increases, subsidy hikes and National Rural Employment Guarantee Act (NREGA) rollout.

This unprecedented splurge of fiscal profligacy may indeed have cushioned the fallout from the global crisis for a year or two. But the composition of the huge expenditure hikes (mainly government pay, subsidies and entitlement programmes) made subsequent retraction politically difficult. As a result, the persisting high fiscal deficits since 2008 have fuelled the long bout of inflation, kept interest rates high, reduced public savings and fed the rising CAD.

Exchange Rate Mismanagement Since 2009

Although senior government spokesmen tend to project India's external deficit pressures as a recent problem, in fact, the CAD has been consistently above the Prime Minister's 'safe benchmark' of 2.5 per cent of GDP since 2009-10. That means we are in the fifth year of a dangerously high CAD. A significant contributory factor has been the authorities' (government plus Reserve Bank of India [RBI]) shift since spring 2009 to a relatively 'hand off' policy towards the rupee's exchange rate. So, when capital inflows recovered since 2009, the rupee was allowed to appreciate sharply in 2009 and 2010, despite a clearly rising CAD. As some of us pointed out then, the authorities should have instead followed the well-tested, pre-2008 policy of limiting appreciation and building reserves through dollar purchases by the RBI. The failure to do this led to an overvalued rupee, which weakened India's international competiveness and helped fuel the pattern of rising external deficits that now haunt the economy.

The Supply Shocks of 2010-2012

These were multiple, all reflecting policy and governance weaknesses. They include the sudden and damaging tightening of environmental regulations in 2010; the eruption of serious scams in 2G telecom spectrum allocation, coal block allocations and various land scams (all with roots in earlier years) and their debilitating aftermaths in the impacted sectors; the sweeping judicial restraints on iron ore mining in Karnataka and Goa; the fiasco of missing coal and gas supply for many thousand megawatts of freshly completed power projects; the anti-investment tax measures of the 2012 budget; and the generalised 'policy paralysis' in regard to activation, completion and clearances of major projects. All these supply problems reduced production, investment and growth, and some also directly hurt the external balance, as in the case of coal and iron ore.

While each of these supply-side problems had distinct characteristics and policy histories, together they constituted a major (and persisting) supply shock to the Indian economy.

The Neglect of Manufacturing

In marked contrast to the great majority of emerging nations, the share of manufacturing in GDP has stagnated at around 15-17 per cent for decades in India. While the problem is long-standing, the failure to enhance the share during the past decade was a significant contributory factor in the current economic crisis. In the high growth period, 2003-2011, services (including construction) accounted for well over 70 per cent of all growth, while industry (essentially manufacturing and mining) accounted for less than 20 per cent. This lopsided pattern could not sustain high growth for long, and hasn't once services expansion started to flag. The major policy impediments to industrial growth have been unreformed rigidities in the labour market, growing impediments to land acquisition and the continuing weaknesses in infrastructure, especially power, roads, railways and ports. Slow industrial growth has led to limited growth of jobs for low-skilled labour and a steady widening of the merchandise trade deficit, which, in turn, widened the CAD.

Faulty Monetary Policies of July 2013

As everyone knows, between 15 and 23 July, the RBI announced draconian (if somewhat opaque) monetary measures, which effectively increased the short-term policy rates by 300 basis points and sharply reduced liquidity. The measures were taken ostensibly to defend the falling rupee by restricting 'speculation'. The diagnosis was fundamentally incorrect. The rupee was not weakening due to short-run 'speculation', but because of a persisting high CAD, mounting short-term, external debt obligations, and changes in the global environment for capital flows.

So the cure had little connection with the disease. As predicted, the measures did not solve the rupee's weakness; the rupee was trading at a lower value by end July compared to 14 July. Instead, these measures significantly increased interest rates across the entire term structure, curtailed credit growth for productive purposes, made government borrowing more difficult and costly, weakened the health of banks (especially government banks) and, above all, further dampened the outlook for recovery in output and investment. In the process, the policy steps may have inadvertently increased the incentives for withdrawal of equity investments by FIIs (foreign institutional investors) in the Indian stock market, thus adding to the rupee's weakness. Although described as 'temporary', there is little prospect of reversal. The damage has been done and will continue.

Even a quick perusal of the above list of major policy errors suggests that it will take a lot of time and work to repair the damage done to the economy—even more if further unsound policies are adopted, such as tighter import restrictions. So, the outlook for the rupee remains volatile with a downward bias.

---

08 August 2013.

19

Recovery: This Time Will Be Harder

It may seem premature to be discussing a recovery from India's current economic crisis when economic growth has collapsed to 4.4 per cent and is still slowing, manufacturing output is actually falling, job losses are mounting, consumer inflation remains high, the rupee and external finances are still very stressed and the fiscal deficit continues to widen (over 60 per cent of the full year estimate in the first third of the fiscal year). Most investment banks and multilateral agencies are now pegging GDP (gross domestic product) growth for 2013-14 at or around a dismal 4 per cent. Nevertheless, with a bit of luck and a dash of optimism one could envisage the current year as the nadir of this crisis and begin to focus on the shape of the post-crisis recovery.

The last time the Indian economy was in a comparable mess was in 1991, 22 years ago. Then, as we all remember, the newly formed Rao-Singh government launched a programme of stabilisation and structural reforms which helped restore economic buoyancy with remarkable alacrity. GDP growth, which had plummeted to 1.4 per cent in 1991-92, rebounded to 5.4 per cent in 1992-93 and accelerated steadily to average over 7.0 per cent in the three years 1994/95-1996/97. If something similar could be engineered in the coming years, we could easily revert to 9.0 per cent plus growth by 2016. Alas, the likelihood of such a strong recovery looks vanishingly small. Let me outline some of the reasons for this bearish outlook.

Global Economic Environment

Although 1991 was a bad year for the world economy thanks to the 'first Gulf War', the associated oil price spike, the break-up of the Soviet empire and the dot.com bust, global economic fortunes recovered quickly during the US-led 'Clinton boom' of 1992 onwards, providing a strong, supportive backdrop to India's reform efforts. Today, despite some recent optimism, the strength and durability of the United States (US) recovery is still debatable, Europe remains mired in near-recessionary conditions, Japan's recovery is still modest and China's growth has slowed. It is very unlikely that the next five years of world economic growth will come near the record of 1992-1997. Global liquidity will almost certainly tighten and interest rates increase. So, India's recovery will probably have to contend with a less favourable external environment than in the 1990s.

Tractability of the Reform Agenda

The economic reforms of the early 1990s were wide-ranging and potent. Fortunately, some of the key ones could be implemented through administrative action by a determined central government: industrial decontrol, opening up to foreign trade and investment, the switch to a market-based exchange rate regime, the lifting of financial repression, major tax reforms and so on. Contrast this with the so-called 'second generation reforms' that have been stalled for years and need to be implemented to revive strong, sustained growth of the Indian economy. They include: reform of overly rigid labour laws; revamping of the policy and regulatory framework for key infrastructure and energy sectors; major redesign of urban policy; serious reforms of the public education and health systems and so forth.

These reforms, though necessary, are difficult to design and implement and often require hard-to-achieve legislative action. That is one reason they have been waiting in the wings for so long. Moreover, they generally need active cooperation and coordination between central and state governments, ingredients which have proven elusive in an increasingly fractious polity. So the prospects for early and coherent implementation of the necessary reforms are not too good, to put it mildly.

Political Appetite and Administrative
Capacity to Implement Reforms

A related issue is the weak political support for the agenda of economic reforms and the absence of adequate consensus and capacity in the technocracy. In the 1990s, there was widespread support and appreciation for the reforms in crucial segments of the central government technocracy, including the finance ministry, the Prime Minister's office, the ministries of commerce and industry and the Reserve Bank of India (RBI). Such support had been nurtured by a series of reports produced by high-level official committees in the late 1980s, which helped ensure familiarity and buy-in for the reform agenda. So, once the political decisions to undertake reforms had been catalysed by crisis, coordinated implementation could be pursued with considerable success.

At present, it is hard to discern a comparable degree of familiarity and support for the necessary reform agenda in the key central government agencies, let alone the state governments which would need to be involved. In the absence of such techno-administrative consensus, it is hardly surprising that the political commitment is also weak, especially given the unusual weakness of the current political executive. Coherent and decisive policymaking is complicated by the growing role of non-governmental players, ranging from civil society groups to crony capitalists. Ergo, the prospects for strong reforms are also dim for these reasons.

Baggage of Recent History

Quite apart from the low, politico-administrative tractability of the reforms necessary to revive growth, the burden of recent history may also retard a swift recovery. In particular, the last few years' proliferation of ill-designed but expensive entitlement programmes will pre-empt fiscal space for more genuinely developmental public expenditure and challenge macro stability. The recent law on land acquisition will further burden an industrial sector seriously damaged by anti-industry policies, including misguided exchange rate appreciation and capricious tax measures.

Put differently, where will growth of output and employment come from in the years ahead? In the last 15 years, services have been the main engine of overall economic growth. Perhaps inevitably, that engine has begun to sputter and may be hard to reactivate. The prolonged neglect of manufacturing has to be swiftly reversed and supportive policies deployed. The recent rupee depreciation offers substantial encouragement to import substitution and exports. But to fully exploit these opportunities, it is vital to have supportive infrastructure, tax and labour market policies.

All things considered, the outlook for a strong and sustained recovery from the ongoing crisis is not very promising. Almost certainly, it will not match the speedy resurgence from the 1991 crisis. If 2013-14 really does turn out to be the nadir of the present crisis—and there is no guarantee of that—it may be realistic to expect economic growth in the ensuing three years to average around 5-7 per cent.

12 September 2013.

20

From Anxiety to Complacency in Six Weeks?

Hardly six weeks ago, a sense of grim crisis pervaded India's economic policymaking circles and much of the public at large. The underlying causes are well-known: the post-2011 collapse of growth and investor confidence, major problems in infrastructure and energy sectors, persistently high inflation, shrinking job opportunities, and large fiscal and external account deficits. The alarm bell that had most strongly signalled (and reflected) the onset of economic crisis was the plummeting value of the rupee, which had dropped from around ₹53-54 per US$ in May to nearly ₹69/$ by end-August. The rupee's free fall had occurred despite a wide range of measures to reduce gold imports, restrict external payments and drastically tighten monetary policy.

The tide began to turn in early September with the new Reserve Bank of India (RBI) governor's confident and well-considered initial policy statement on 4 September, including the announcement of swap facilities to banks for fresh FCNR (B) deposits of maturity 3 years and over at a rate of 3.5 per cent per year. This quasi exchange rate guarantee soon triggered fresh inflows. Within days of this initiative, wobbles in the US economic recovery suggested possible postponement of the US Federal Reserve's (Fed) pre-announced intentions of 'tapering' its monthly QE (quantitaive easing) liquidity injections, a likelihood that was duly fulfilled by the Fed's 18 September announcement and restored a 'risk on' posture towards emerging markets. India's July and August trade data were also encouraging. Together, these developments ensured a significant recovery in the forex and capital markets, with the rupee climbing back the 62-63 range to the dollar by 20 September.

As currency and financial markets recovered, the sense of crisis and urgency dissipated swiftly. By early October, the senior government officials were reportedly exuding confidence that the currency turbulence was over, the FY (financial year) 2013-14 CAD (current account deficit) would be held below $ 70 billion (around 3.7% of GDP [gross domestic product]) thanks to a sharp decline in legal gold imports (August onwards) and some recovery in exports, the centre's fiscal deficit would not cross the "red line" of the budgeted 4.8 per cent of GDP, and economic growth would recover to average about 5.5 per cent of GDP for the full year, despite the 4.4 per cent rate recorded in the June quarter. Confidence is certainly commendable but when does it shade into complacency? Let us consider the realism of these official macroeconomic expectations.

If the sharp decline in gold imports in recent weeks persists, it would certainly help scale back the CAD. A significant question is how much has this decline in gold imports through official channels been substituted by an increase in smuggled gold? As we know from the high levels of smuggled imports in the pre-1990s era, these are typically associated with financing arrangements which tend to reduce the recorded levels of invisible earnings and capital inflows, thus offsetting the apparent gain in the trade deficit. Another major imponderable is the impact of the ongoing US government shutdown and possible failure to raise the debt ceiling. On the one hand, such uncertainties are likely to prolong current levels of QE and thus ease the financing of India's CAD. On the other, a significant setback to US and global economic activity could damp exports of goods and services and reignite global financial turmoil. It is impossible to assess the net effects on India's external accounts at this stage.

The government's expectation of 5.5 per cent growth this year looks decidedly optimistic. Aside from a good, monsoon-propelled performance in agriculture (which accounts for only 15% of India's GDP) and a modest recent uptick in some core sectors (from depressed levels) and some exports, it is hard to locate signs of a significant resurgence in economic activity. On the contrary, various business surveys (such as by CII-ASCON) point to continued doldrums in industry. Major sub-sectors such as automobiles, consumer durables, textiles and construction are still in negative territory. Perhaps more significantly, the latest HSBC PMI (Purchasing Managers Index) data for September shows a sharp contraction in the hugely important services sector, with the index falling below 45 (index values below 50 indicate negative growth outlook). The PMI for manufacturing and services combined fell to 46, the lowest level in four and a half years. It is hardly surprising that the projections by foreign and domestic financial institutions (including the International Monetary Fund [IMF]) cluster in the range of 4.0 to 4.5 per cent growth in 2013-14, that is, even lower than in the previous year and the lowest in 11 years.

The most implausible element in the finance ministry's present confident/complacent macro expectations pertains to the fiscal deficit target of 4.8 per cent of GDP. As we know from the recently published fiscal accounts for August, the fiscal deficit in the first five months of the year already accounted for 75.0 per cent of the full year target. In contrast, tax revenues were just over 20.0 per cent of the yearly total, while non-debt capital receipts (mainly from disinvestment) were less than 10.0 per cent. There is little prospect of huge buoyancy in these receipts in the second half of the year. On the expenditure side, subsidies will overshoot significantly because of higher rupee prices for oil and fertiliser imports, unless prices are raised soon. Two or three weeks back, there were strong rumours about a ₹4-5/litre increase in diesel prices. But these have subsided and such price rises look increasingly improbable with major state elections due next month and the general elections by May. For similar reasons the sharp curtailment of other budgeted expenditures of the kind done last year look much less feasible this year.

In sum, the fiscal deficit could be overshot by significant margin by the time fiscal year ends. In the first five months of FY 2013-14, the centre's fiscal deficit ratio has been running at a whopping 8.7 per cent of GDP. Bringing it down to 4.8 per cent in the remaining seven months looks impossibly difficult; without recourse to seriously creative accounting ploys. In any case, it is worth pointing out that a deficit which stays high through most of the year imposes the associated costs of higher inflation, higher interest rates, more crowding out of private investment and greater pressure on CAD during the period, even if 'miraculously' corrected in the final months. It is also worth emphasising that if the months unfold without any serious policies to correct the deficit, there is a growing risk of negative external perceptions (including a possible credit rating downgrade), which could have serious adverse consequences on external financing of the CAD and on currency markets.

In other words, India's macroeconomic condition remains quite shaky and certainly does not warrant an iota of complacency. This is doubly true if one considers the available patchy data on employment trends, which point to miserable job prospects for the country's burgeoning youth population.

---

10 October 2013.

21

Economic Management in Pre-election Months?

The national elections are hardly six months away and a series of state elections will span the next few weeks. In the best of circumstances this would be a challenging period for economic management, as the political executive focuses increasingly on trying to win the elections and the 'professional economic managers' (senior civil servants, the central banking elite and their advisers) try to insulate the economy from some of the worst excesses of political 'short-termism'. These tensions are amplified greatly in the present situation when the Indian economy is performing poorly: growth is low, inflation is high, employment is stagnant and both domestic and external finances are under serious stress. Both groups, the 'politicos' and the 'professionals', would like to see the economy perform better in the short run, but the former are much more inclined to undertake measures (or postpone desirable 'bullet-biting' steps) for politically visible short-term gains at the expense of longer-term costs.

One can readily imagine some of the short-run political priorities (not necessarily consistent): no more administrative price increases; inflation in widely consumed goods and services should be reduced, or, at least, contained to a minimum; spending on welfare programmes must be maintained or increased; the rupee must not depreciate (further); private investment and employment should be stimulated… and so forth. The subtexts, often unstated, include: don't worry about the fiscal deficit, nobody knows what that is; and don't worry about economic reforms (or even economic growth) in the months ahead, they will not affect the election outcome. Just ensure there are no critical shortages or currency collapses.

Let us explore the emerging dilemmas with respect to a few key macroeconomic issues.

Inflation and Growth

Normally, both high growth and low inflation are the two most important objectives of macroeconomic policy for any government. The problem (and paradox) is that for the six months remaining before the general elections, the outcomes on both these yardsticks are largely 'baked in the cake' already. They will reflect mainly the wisdom (or folly) of policies undertaken in preceding months and years. Not much can be done through policies to affect outcomes in the brief time remaining. Thus, the projections outlined a fortnight back in the Reserve Bank of India's (RBI) monetary policy statement are good approximations of what will be recorded by the end of FY 2013-14: GDP (gross domestic product) growth of 5 per cent, WPI (wholesale price index) inflation of 6.0 per cent plus and CPI (consumer price index) inflation of 9.0 per cent plus. Possibly, economic growth may turn out to be a little lower, closer to 4.5 per cent.

These are not happy economic numbers with which to enter the national electoral contest. But there they are. It is true that more energetic and effective efforts by the cabinet committee on investments to break logjams with stalled projects may affect growth, but the rewards are likely to come later, beyond the six-month horizon. This assessment may reduce the incentives to work hard and effectively to relieve the present constraints, but the negative consequences of inactivity will be incurred later too.

Nor will a burst of loose monetary policy achieve a ramping up of growth in the short run, though it will certainly worsen current high levels of inflation soon enough. Indeed, in these pre-election months, the RBI may have a freer mandate to pursue a tighter monetary policy without the usual pressures and pleas from the government side for lower interest rates. Within the range of realistic options, higher policy rates may help to contain inflationary pressures in the short run without significant damage to growth.

Fiscal Balance

What about the temptation to ramp up pre-election spending in a last mile dash to win nation-wide votes? The truth is, fortunately, it is too late for that. No new populist programme can be launched and made effective in remaining few months. Of course, higher than budgeted spending on subsidies and welfare programmes is certainly possible. Here there are real choices and dilemmas. Despite the Finance Minister's (and the Ministry's) oft-repeated pronouncements of a 'red line' commitment to honour the 4.8 per cent of GDP fiscal deficit target, the likelihood of overshooting is high. In the first half of 2013-14 the fiscal deficit has been running at about 8.0 per cent of GDP, thanks mainly to major shortfalls in budgeted tax and non-tax revenues as well as disinvestment receipts. To compress this run-rate down to 4.8 per cent by year-end will require fairly draconian expenditure restraints, or substantial creative accounting (such as postponement of subsidy payment obligations and tax refunds into the following year) or a combination of both.

Substantial postponement of government payment obligations is almost certain since they will be seen to relatively costless in the short run. However, sharp expenditure cuts could have some negative political fallout. They would not be undertaken if our external finances were in better shape. But they are not. So, a major, transparent overshooting of fiscal targets could heighten the risks of a credit-rating downgrade, leading to additional downward pressure on the rupee during a politically sensitive period. Hence the government is likely to be somewhat serious on expenditure restraint, though perhaps not enough to credibly achieve the 4.8 per cent of GDP budget target. Let us see.

Rupee and External Finances

That brings us to the principal vulnerability in pre-election economic management: the continuing precariousness of our external finances. If there was any doubt on this score, it has surely been dispelled by the rupee's 3.0 per cent depreciation in the last week after a lull of several weeks' stability. The main proximate cause appears to have been the publication of strong employment figures and other recent signs of strength in the US recovery, which, in turn, has triggered speculation about an early start to the famous "tapering" of the US Federal Reserve's $85 billion a month quantitative easing programme. What must worry the government most is that the rupee's wobble occurred despite continuing, extraordinary inflows under the new (since September), FCNR (B) swapped facility and the end-August arrangements to keep the bulk of oil import bills of the petroleum refiners off the spot forex market.

One likely response may be to announce a continuation of the FCNR (B) swap facilities beyond 30 November (the earlier date for cessation of the facility). That may well be the political preference of a pre-election government. But it comes with the heavy costs of a continuing exchange guarantee (which is what the RBI's swap facilities amount to), which will surely impose a substantial fiscal burden in the future. A better response would be to accept the rupee depreciation catalysed by a change in tapering expectations. Tapering will happen sooner or later and we have to adjust to that hard fact.

Clearly, the next few months are going to test the mettle and wisdom of both the 'politicos' and the 'professionals'.

---

14 November 2013.

22

UPA's Economic Legacy
Good, Bad or Ugly?

With the 15th Lok Sabha having ended and the next general elections two months away, it is timely to assess the Gandhi-Singh led United Progressive Alliance (UPA) government's economic legacy after 10 years of its rule. If one takes the decade of UPA rule as a whole and looks at a few key economic indicators, it is possible to claim, at first glance, that this government's achievements are good, perhaps even very good. After all, overall economic growth has averaged 7.5 per cent per year, the fastest in any decade in India's history. This rapid growth in GDP has raised average income, as reflected by per capita national income, by nearly 75.0 per cent in real, inflation-adjusted rupees. This too is the highest decadal increase in average income in India's history. Turning to poverty, the latest official data show that the percentage of the population below the poverty line (Tendulkar definition) has dropped sharply from 37.0 per cent in 2004-05 to 22.0 per cent in 2011-12. It is the steepest decline in the poverty ratio ever seen in India.

Unfortunately, there are at least three broad sets of reasons why such a favourable assessment does not stand up to scrutiny. First, most of the high growth occurred in the first seven years up to 2010-2011 (averaging 8.5% a year), after which economic growth crashed, mainly because of the accumulation of bad economic policies pursued by the government. In both the two most recent years, 2012-13 and 2013-14, official estimates show that GDP growth was below 5.0 per cent, the first time this has happened in two successive years in the last quarter of a century. Industrial production has plummeted to zero in the last two years. Even the buoyant service sectors of the economy have slowed significantly. Inflation in consumer prices has jumped and remained high (9-11% a year) in the last five years. The foreign trade and current account deficits rose steadily and dangerously since

2008-09 and triggered two bouts of sharp exchange rate depreciation (in 2011 and 2013). The golden years of high growth with financial stability are long past.

Second, the UPA's economic policies were mediocre to start with and worsened increasingly as the decade evolved. Indeed, the high growth and low inflation of the first five years were due mainly to the global economic boom of 2002-2007 and the wide-ranging, productivity-enhancing economic reforms carried out prior to 2004. The sole, important, growth-supporting UPA policy was the major fiscal consolidation achieved between 2004-05 and 2007-08. And this major policy achievement was wholly squandered in 2008-09, through pre-election ramping up of major subsidies (oil, food and fertiliser), entitlement programmes (such as NREGA), government pay and other sops. The subsequent persistence with "fiscal populism" and the associated high fiscal and revenue deficits, kept inflation and interest rates high and helped widen the external account deficits to dangerous levels.

Amongst the other most noteworthy macro, sectoral and governance failures of the government were:

- the perpetuation of laws and policies, which hugely discouraged new employment in the organised sector, thus condemning over 95.0 per cent of the young new entrants to the labour force (the so-called demographic dividend) to low-paid, insecure occupations in the unorganised or informal sector of the economy;

- the growing recourse to 'crony-capitalist' policies in key sectors such as telecom (the notorious 2G spectrum allocation scam), mining (coal and iron ore), and land allocation, which have come to light since 2010 and their debilitating aftermaths continue to impact these and related sectors;

- the deliberate appreciation of the rupee in 2009-10 was ill-judged and contributed significantly to the subsequent widening of external deficits as both import-substitution and exports were effectively discouraged;

- the sudden tightening of environmental standards (2010) and the inexplicable recourse to capricious and retrospective tax policies (2012), together with sectoral scams noted above, played havoc with the general investment and business climate and contributed to the sharp economic slowdown;

- the large increases in food procurement prices and a failing public distribution system turned the government into a massive hoarder of foodgrains and ramped up food inflation;

- even the success of inducing record investment in new power generation turned sour because of failures in coordinating fuel linkages (coal and gas) and weak energy pricing policies, leaving many thousands of costly megawatts of generating capacity idle or under-utilised;

- government's focus on entitlements and coverage, along with neglect of quality and accountability, meant that large parts of the massive systems of public education and health were seriously dysfunctional, although here the blame also falls on state governments.

Third, the witches' brew of poor economic performance in recent years and a longer history of bad economic policies have combined to leave an unenviable array of economic vulnerabilities and challenges for whichever government takes office this summer. They include:

- the failure to create reasonably decent jobs for the burgeoning young population of new job-seekers (over 10 million each year), with profound adverse consequences for social and political stability;

- the extraordinary loss of growth momentum in the economy;

- the unprecedented stagnation in manufacturing output, despite the ready availability of cheap, low-skill labour;

- the continue scarcity of good quality, efficient infrastructure (power, roads, ports, railways, water supply and sanitation);

- the heightened vulnerability of agriculture to water stress in large parts of the country;

- the widespread cancer of stalled, incomplete and delayed projects, which have reduced growth and burdened the banking sector with a mountain of dodgy loans that weigh heavily on the viability of many public sector banks and weaken overall financial stability;

- the array of ill-conceived and inefficiently run entitlement programmes (such as rural employment guarantee, food security and education), which achieve limited welfare gains at the cost of enormous stress on fiscal capacity and foregone public investment;

- weak external finances, which are vulnerable to exogenous declines in capital inflows or to normalisation of recently increased gold duties and import restrictions, which have resurrected a rapidly growing trade in *hawala*-financed gold smuggling;

- a legacy of new lows in the quality of central governance (including economic governance), that have further weakened the country's rickety public administration in all areas.

Fundamentally, the decade of UPA government failed to undertake economic, social and administrative reforms to strengthen the India's long-term development potential, despite the golden opportunity offered by the years of high growth and investment. It is hard to resist the conclusion that the overall economic legacy is bad, if not ugly.

13 March 2014.

23

Economic Revival
When and How Strong?

Last month (26 February) I had outlined the dismal economic legacy being bequeathed by 10 years of United Progressive Alliance (UPA) rule to whichever government assumes office after the national elections are completed in May. To recapitulate, in brief, this grim legacy includes:

- a mounting scarcity of decent jobs for the 10 million plus of new entrants to the workforce each year;
- an extraordinary collapse in overall growth momentum of the economy;
- high levels of consumer price inflation for the sixth year running;
- an unprecedented stagnation in industrial activity for two successive years;
- continued scarcity of good, efficient infrastructure;
- a growing problem of water stress in agriculture;
- a big overhang of incomplete and underutilised infrastructure projects, casting a massive burden of weak and non-performing loans on the nation's banking sector;
- a legacy of ill-designed and expensive entitlement programmes and high subsidies, feeding large fiscal deficits and pre-empting resources from more productive public expenditure;
- still weak external sector finances, vulnerable to volatility in capital inflows and foreign trade; and
- a rudderless and demoralised public administrative structure.

Whichever government comes to power after the elections, it will face daunting challenges to revive and sustain economic growth and significantly improve the opportunities for gainful employment.

Clearly, the more coherent and stable the new government, the greater the chance of significant and sustainable economic revival. Many believe that if a Bharatiya Janata Party (BJP)-centred coalition, led by Narendra Modi, assumes power in May, then India's manifold economic ills will be on the way to swift resolution. Even if this political outcome were to transpire (and Indian elections can be full of surprises), the much hoped for economic revival is likely to be gradual and its sustainability dependent on sound policies and supportive circumstances. Consider the following factors.

First, the assumed political outcome would very likely give an initial boost to confidence and 'animal spirits' of both investors and consumers, leading to an uptick of investment and, perhaps, consumption. However, while a revival of confidence is important, it has to be sustained, and that will be hard to do without tackling effectively the key constraints and weaknesses noted above. For example, it is an open question as to how quickly the debilitating backlog of stalled and idle projects can be dealt with. This needs clear political leadership, strong inter-ministerial coordination and determined administrative follow-through. Much will depend on the coherence and politico-administrative strength of the new government, and its ability to re-energise and motivate an administrative structure weakened by years of high-level corruption and bypassing of administrative norms.

Second, even the initial, confidence-inspired boost to investment and consumption may stoke inflationary pressures more than it does growth, if the supply constraints on the latter are not loosened quickly. One way to reduce this danger is to curb the growth of government expenditure (and the fiscal deficit) to make room for productive investment. But this will not be easy given the present government's well-known postponement into the next fiscal year of massive subsidy dues (for oil, food, fertiliser) owed to the relevant public sector companies and agencies, postponements which are already constraining the operational capacities of these entities. There are also likely to be large claims on the fisc for recapitalising several public sector banks, highly stressed by their portfolios of non-performing or dodgy loans, especially to stalled or failing infrastructure companies. And two years down the road, the Seventh Pay Commission's recommendations may impose huge new obligations for central and state governments. Nor does the revenue side of the budget offer much buoyancy without a resurgence of economic growth. Certainly, the projections in the present government's Interim Budget for fiscal 2014-15 look fancifully optimistic.

Third, turning to infrastructure, yes, there is some scope for better performance through resolving current bottlenecks like grossly inadequate fuel supply linkages for power plants, even though it won't be easy to increase production of coal and gas, as the present government has already found. Looking further ahead, who is going to undertake India's massive infrastructure requirements in the next few years? The central government will be strapped for cash, unless the new rulers can drastically reduce the bloated bill for subsidies and hold pay increases in check. That doesn't look very likely given the BJP's track record of legislative support for populist entitlement programmes and other measures such as the recent, new land acquisition act. The last decade has shown that PPPs (public-private partnerships) are a mixed blessing at best, given their requirements for high governance standards and the unfortunate reality of 'crony capitalism'. Besides, nearly all the major private infrastructure companies are saddled with massive debts and low market valuations and in no position to seriously expand operations.

Fourth, the viability of external finances cannot be taken for granted. It is true that the large current account deficit of last year has been successfully managed through tariff increases and restrictions on gold imports, some improvement in the underlying trade account because of currency depreciation and the economic slowdown and the expensive swap facilities deployed by the Reserve Bank last August. Much of this is temporary or non-repeatable. The recent pre-election surge in the stock market (and the rise in the rupee value) has been fed by large inflows of foreign portfolio investment. But all this is easily reversible, if electoral expectations are belied or the new government's economic policies disappoint. And who knows what the evolving crisis in Ukraine will do to oil prices, not to mention other uncertainties in the global arena.

All things considered, the recovery in economic growth is unlikely to be strong, perhaps limited to the 5-6 per cent range in the coming fiscal year. And beyond that, it will depend obviously on the functioning of the new government and its actual economic policies. We have to wait and see.

Finally, the massive problem of too few decent jobs for the millions of low-skilled, new entrants to the work force will continue to grow and bedevil India's economic and social progress, with real prospects of serious social distress, political turbulence and sharply rising crime. East Asian economic history shows the way to the only viable solution to the 'youth bulge', namely, the sustained growth of low-skill, factory-based manufacturing. So far, India has missed that bus thanks to her poor education system, weak infrastructure and ill-conceived labour regulations, which severely discourage fresh employment in organised manufacturing. The prospects for swift and effective improvement in these key policy dimensions are not promising.

13 March 2014.

III

Beyond Crisis

24

More of the Same?

On 9 June 2014, President Pranab Mukherjee delivered the new government's first PA (president's address) to the 16th Lok Sabha. How important are these set-piece speeches? Well, judging by the one delivered by his predecessor almost exactly five years ago when the United Progressive Alliance (UPA) began its second innings, they can be important harbingers of the policies, programmes and priorities of a new government. Recall that in June 2009 after the UPA had won the elections and Congress had greatly improved its seat strength, there was a great deal of hope that UPA II, no longer dependent on Left support for parliamentary majority, would resuscitate the stalled programme of economic reforms. Such hopes were extinguished as the years passed by, helping to land the Indian economy in its current mess of low growth, high inflation, stagnant employment and vulnerable external finances.

A careful reading of Pratibha Patil's PA to Parliament in early June 2009 would have squelched these hopes right in the beginning. As I pointed out then ("the Leviathan Returns", *Business Standard*, 11 June 2009) her address was a clarion call for massive government spending on a broad range of entitlement and other programmes, with hardly a whisper about economic policy reforms. Even job creation, which only got passing mention, was to be the government's direct responsibility, "High growth is necessary to provide the *government* (italics added) the capacity to expand opportunities for employment." Well, we got the massive spending alright along with high and sustained inflation, collapsed growth, a plummeting rupee and shrinking job opportunities...and no reforms. The lesson seems to be that we should take PAs seriously, especially the first one of a new government.

What can one glean from last week's PA about the National Democratic Alliance (NDA) government's priorities for policies and programmes in the new climate of hope and enormous expectations engendered by the recent election outcomes? One would have expected that the PA cleared by the Modi Cabinet would outline fresh new policy priorities to revive growth and employment. One might have also expected strong words of encouragement for the private sector and a statement of intentions to free up onerous restrictions on land and labour markets. Well, such expectations were largely confounded. Indeed, what is startling are the similarities with the UPA II PA of June 2009. The new PA spends most of its 38 paragraphs (out of 50 total) about economic and social matters on government programmes such as the Pradhan Mantri Krishi Sinchayee Yojana for water management, IITs (Indian Institute of Technology) and IIMs (Indian Institute of Management) in every state, a National Multi-Skill Mission, a National Health Assurance Mission, a "Swachh Bharat Mission" for sanitation, a "Van Bandhu Kalyan Yojana" for tribals, a broadband highway to reach every village, Dedicated Freight Corridors and Industrial Corridors, a Diamond Quadrilateral for high-speed trains, the Sagar Mala project for ports, 100 new cities with world class amenities (what about the 8,000 existing cities and towns with poor amenities where India's urban citizens currently dwell?), a new Ganga cleansing programme, a mission mode project for 50 tourist circuits...and so on.

Like the PA of 2009, it's all about government programmes and spending; and very little about policy reforms. Indeed, given its language and content, last week's PA could have been comfortably crafted by the recently defeated UPA government! (So what was the election all about?) The obvious question is where will the money for these programmes come from, especially bearing in mind the large needs of under-capitalised public sector banks and our under-equipped armed forces? From even higher fiscal deficits with their demonstrably pernicious effects on inflation, growth and external balance? Individually, most of these projects, programmes and missions may seem quite worthy. But as a government's overall programme, in the current dire straits of the Indian economy, they hardly seem to match the needs of the times.

Another eerie similarity between Mukherjee's PA and Patil's is that both pay little attention to the paramount challenge of job creation that confronts India's young and burgeoning labour force. It is only in paragraph 27 that we find, "For rapid creation of jobs in the manufacturing sector, the government will strategically promote labour-intensive manufacturing. Employment opportunities will also be expanded by promoting tourism and agro-based industries." Beware the word 'promote' in policy documents. It usually means either expensive tax incentives or the writer doesn't have much clue about the real policy requirements. In this case, as many years of development history has amply demonstrated, India has little chance of replicating East Asian success with growing labour-intensive manufacturing without a serious overhaul of our highly job-destructive labour laws. And there is little chance of any kind of manufacturing surging ahead without significant amendments to the recently enacted land acquisition law. Not that the PA mentions any of this.

The big puzzle is why does Mukherjee's PA appear to be a close cousin of Patil's 2009 speech? Didn't the drafters (including the Modi cabinet) want to differentiate their approach to social and economic policy from the ill-judged one followed by the UPA government? Couldn't they have used this opportunity to have the President point out the exceptionally weak economic and financial conditions inherited from the bumbling UPA government and the tough and far-reaching decisions now required to undo the past damage and take the country forward? Is it simply a case of 'bureaucratic capture' by civil servant drafters who look at past PAs and the relevant election manifestos and cobble together 50 paragraphs? Judging by recent press reports, Prime Minister Modi has been quite forthright in emphasising the poor economic health of the country and the need for tough and unpopular economic and financial corrective actions. It is a pity his clarity and candour were not reflected in last week's PA. It might have been wise to have the President forewarn all members of Parliament of the difficult choices and decisions necessitated by the UPA's bad economic legacy. Hope is a wonderful sentiment. But it cannot substitute for hard analysis and even harder corrective actions.

Now let us see what mixture of hope, realism and courage the NDA's first budget unveils.

---

18 June 2014.

25

Budget 2014
Good Beginning or Missed Opportunity?

By now reams have been written on first budget of the new National Democratic Alliance (NDA) government, led by Narendra Modi, presented on 10 July 2014. There is really nothing new left to say. But a regular columnist is duty-bound to pen his bit. So here goes. Any Union Budget is a massive and complex document. No fair comprehensive assessment is possible in a single column. So I will pick a few issues for comment.

Could it Have Been a 'Big Bang' Budget?

This one clearly wasn't. Contrary to widespread expectations, fuelled by the election campaign and the decisive victory, there was no paradigm shift or breakaway from the pattern of the last few budgets. No really major economic reforms (such as of labour and land laws) were announced. Despite the inherited fiscal mess, no surgical changes were proposed for expenditure (level or composition) or taxes. The UPA government's architecture of costly and inefficient entitlement programmes and subsidies survive unscathed. And there is no radical reform of tax policy. The excuse those 45 days was not enough to attempt bold departures does not wash. Manmohan Singh's paradigm-shifting 1991 budget had comparable preparatory time. True, that radical budget was presented in the midst of a BoP (balance of payments) crisis. But this budget also came at a time of quasi-crisis, with industry stagnant for two years, years of high consumer inflation, depressed investment, rising unemployment and low economic growth. What's more, this budget was presented by the freshly mandated NDA with development (*vikas*) as its central plank. The time was surely ripe for bold departures. However, continuity has trumped change.

Obviously, a conscious political choice was made to present a middle of the road budget as a "beginning of the journey towards sustained growth of 7-8 per cent," to quote minister Jaitley's words, although this did not entirely square with his characterisation of "the Budget is the most comprehensive action plan" for the journey ahead. The problem with this choice is that the opportunity for a 'big bang' budget is unlikely to occur again. Today the blame for the current economic mess could be rightly laid at the door of the previous government's economic mismanagement to justify radical corrective steps now. By next year, perhaps earlier, the performance and problems of the economy will 'belong' to the NDA and so will the political cost of any 'tough decisions'. So a one-time opportunity has been foregone.

Some Budget Pluses and Minuses

Like all middle of the road budgets, this one has its pluses and minuses. Notable among the former are the announced reforms in tax administration (especially the provisions for advance rulings and transfer pricing), the proposed increases in FDI (foreign direct investment) caps to 49 per cent for insurance and defence production (though it is doubtful that foreign arms suppliers will, as investors with minority stake, transfer the necessary technology), the focus on infrastructure sectors through various modalities, the renewed commitment to expeditiously implement GST (goods and services tax) and the commitment (how strong?) to overhaul the major subsidies on petroleum, food and urea, which today far exceed the central government's total capital expenditure.

Amongst the negatives are the proliferation of ₹100 crore down payments for a bewildering variety of new government projects and programmes ('the band of 29'), the extensive tinkering with customs and excise rates (the former mainly protectionist and the latter complicating the transition to unified GST rates), the enormous faith in PPPs (public-private partnerships) (despite their track record of widespread problems in contracting and execution), and, despite assurances, a fresh transgression of retrospective taxation for existing unit holders of debt mutual funds, most of whom are probably individuals and not corporates as claimed in the minister's speech.

Two larger issues are elaborated below.

Fiscal Stance

Minister Jaitley very deliberately committed the government to a fiscal deficit target of 4.1 per cent of GDP (gross domestic product), the same number as in his predecessor, Chidambaram's Interim Budget. This may prove unwise. The Interim budget's numbers had been widely critiqued as far too optimistic on revenue mobilisation. By adopting almost the same revenue targets, Jaitley has to face the same scepticism. How can tax revenues grow at nearly 20.0 per cent when GDP is assumed to grow at 13.0 per cent in nominal terms? How can income (non-corporate) tax revenues grow at 27.0 per cent and services tax revenues increase by 31.0 per cent? The targets for non-tax revenues also look high. It is one thing to set challenging targets and quite another to adopt unrealistic ones. Would it not have been wiser to set more reasonable (and yet challenging) targets for revenue mobilisation, even if that meant a fiscal deficit target of 4.4 per cent or so? Less impressive perhaps for immediate fiscal consolidation, but probably carrying more credibility for both this year and later years. After all, if the actual fiscal deficit for 2014-15 ends closer to 4.4 per cent of GDP, it not only undermines the government's fiscal credibility for the current year but also raises doubts about future budgetary projections.

Besides, from an economic standpoint, with continued slow growth, there may well be merit in actually running a slightly higher fiscal deficit than the one copied from the Interim budget.

Whatever Happened to Privatisation?

If the budget is any guide, the new NDA government displays a more statist policy stance than Vajpayee's government (NDA1). The latter undertook quite a few successful privatisations of public sector enterprises. And it did so quite openly. The new government (NDA2) seems closer to the UPA mould, hesitant even to use the word 'disinvestment' in the budget speech and seemingly uncomfortable with privatisation or strategic sales of government enterprises.

This stance is confirmed in Jaitley's paragraphs relating bank capitalisation, where public sector banks are encouraged to raise more capital through the market to help meet their Basel-III norms, but subject to the condition that the "government will continue to have majority shareholding" in these banks. This is in sharp contrast to NDA1's tabling of legislation in Parliament to reduce the floor level of government ownership from the extant one of 51.0 per cent to 33.0 per cent. The 51.0 per cent constraint will make it much harder to capitalise public sector banks without heavy support from the budget, whether in this or future years.

So what's the bottom line? Clearly the new government has adopted an incremental, non-radical approach in budget-making, preferring continuity over change. That may (or may not) be politically astute. It almost certainly ensures that India's economic ills will take longer to cure than if a bolder approach had been taken. 'Achche din' ahead? May be, but we will have to wait longer for the revival of growth and jobs…and perhaps endure inflation and economic vulnerability for longer too.

Now let us see what mixture of hope, realism and courage the NDA's first budget unveils.

16 July 2014.

26

Policies Awaited

lmost three months have passed since the National Democratic Alliance (NDA) government, Mark II, was sworn in. Since then, there have been three major programmatic statements by the government: the President's Address to the first session of the 16th Lok Sabha in June, the Finance Minister's budget speech of July and, last week, and the Prime Minister's widely acclaimed Independence Day address to the nation from the ramparts of the Red Fort. Naturally, all three had significant economic content. And there have been nearly three months of governmental administrative and legislative action.

What have we learnt about the government's economic policy priorities from all this? By policy priorities I mean the actual policies, not the standard objectives of high growth in output and employment, low inflation, sustainable external balance, better social indicators of education and health, improved environment, good governance and so on, which are normally the stated objectives of all governments all over the world. Well, the answer, in a nutshell, is not as much we might have wished.

As I pointed out then (Chapter 24), the President's address was devoted mainly to a list of the new government's expenditure programme intentions, such as broadband highways to villages and 100 smart new cities, and revealed little about the government's policy programme. Last month's budget was a middle-of-the-road, incrementalist budget, lacking the kind of paradigm-shifting announcement of new policies (that many had hoped for) to deal with the dismal economic scene inherited from the previous government (my budget assessment in *Business Standard,* 16 July 2014). The Prime Minister's 15 August address was undoubtedly inspirational and outlined important economic and social objectives, such as making India a global hub for manufacturing, ensuring bank accounts for all poor families, major thrusts in sanitation and cleanliness and a radical restructuring of the Planning Commission. However, the policies and road maps to achieve these worthy goals remain to be articulated.

Another way to understand and assess the policy priorities of the NDA government is to focus on the key policy weaknesses of the previous government (which led to India's current economic malaise) and to try and discern the extent to which the NDA government has initiated or announced necessary policy shifts to improve economic outcomes. Some of the significant ones are listed below:

(a) Fiscal consolidation: Although the July budget proposed a modest reduction of the central government fiscal deficit in 2014-15 compared to the previous year, this does not appear attainable, given the overly optimistic projections for tax and non-tax revenues. Nor has there been any significant restructuring of entitlements, subsidies and other expenditure programmes, although an Expenditure Reforms Commission has been now established to recommend measures before the next budget. Hence the negative effects of a large fiscal deficit on inflation and interest rates continue.

(b) Anti-inflation Policy: At an y-o-y rate of 8.0 per cent in July 2014, consumer prices inflation remains uncomfortably high, entirely justifying the Reserve Bank of India's (RBI) reluctance to start reducing policy interest rates. Although the NDA government has begun some open market sales of food grains to moderate prices, the amounts have been modest, given the 70 million tonnes of high cost public stocks available. Systematic efforts to reform India's highly distorted system of food procurement, stocking and distribution are yet to be announced.

(c) Exchange rate policy: Given India's continued high rate of consumer price inflation (relative to trading partners), the real effective exchange rate of the rupee has again been appreciating in recent months (after the sharp depreciations of last summer), pointing to prospects of growing trade and current account deficits in future, especially if the present restrictive policies on gold imports are normalised. More active currency intervention by the RBI to prevent undue rupee appreciation is called for.

(d) Policy Paralysis: The well-known and widely-prevalent 'policy paralysis' and despondency in the last two years of the previous government has given way to a strong sense of confidence and hope based on the single-party majority secured by the Bharatiya Janata Party (BJP) in the recent national election and the strong leadership associated with Prime Minister Modi. Capital inflows and stock markets have surged and business confidence surveys indicate a revival of 'animal spirits'. The government has also streamlined decision-making by abolishing Groups of Ministers, strengthening the Prime Minister's Office, speeding up environmental clearances and pushing for greater accountability across government offices. However the impact of all this on the massive backlog of stalled and incomplete projects is as yet unclear.

(e) Employment and Manufacturing: The Prime Minister has strongly and rightly emphasised the critical importance of the manufacturing sector for both reviving economic growth and providing vitally necessary employment opportunities for India's burgeoning youth population (with over 10 million new entrants to the labour force each year). However, the national polices required to bring about this resuscitation of manufacturing have yet to be announced or put in place in the critical areas of labour laws, land acquisition law, infrastructure and skilling of the workforce. The Rajasthan government has taken an interesting and potentially important lead in amending labour laws to encourage greater employment. Whether this will lead to widespread emulation or similar central government legislative initiatives remains to be seen. On the onerous provisions of the new land acquisition law crafted by the previous government, the NDA government has begun a process of consultations with the states; the outcome is not yet known.

(f) Infrastructure and Energy: The depth and breadth of the disarray in policies and performance of key infrastructure and energy sectors in recent years is well-known. For example, over 20,000 megawatts of new power generation stands idle for want of adequate supplies of coal and gas, burdening banks with massive non-performing assets and forcing electricity users to turn to high cost diesel gensets. National highway construction has slowed to a crawl for lack of timely land acquisition, environmental constraints or breakdown of PPP (private-public partnership) agreements. Railway finances and capital equipment are very weak. Oil and gas development are plagued by problems of pricing, subsidy-burdened national majors and various contract disputes. The new government is trying to grapple with these deep-seated problems through more effective governmental coordination and follow-through. However, the situation also calls for far-reaching reforms of electricity, gas, coal and oil pricing and restructuring of public sector monopoly producers/suppliers. Such new policies are awaited.

(g) Public Sector Banks (PSBs): With 70 per cent of all bank deposits, PSBs remain dominant in the country's banking system. However, past policies have led to high ratios of non-performing assets and low levels of capitalisation. The governance framework for PSBs calls for urgent reforms. PSBs will also need to access capital markets to meet the impending Basel-III norms. But the Finance Minister has stated his opposition to facilitating this through amendment of banking laws to allow government ownership to fall below 51.0 per cent.

To sum up, the NDA government has yet to articulate its policy priorities and initiatives in major areas of the economy needing urgent attention. Until this is done and hard policy choices made, it is unlikely that India's economic growth will revive to the 7.0 per cent plus levels experienced in 2003-2011. The expansion of employment opportunities will remain correspondingly sluggish.

---

20 August 2014.

27

Where is Team Modi

The past few weeks have witnessed an extraordinary demonstration of energy, oratory, skilful projection of personal authority, high diplomacy and popular showmanship by Prime Minister (PM) Narendra Modi. At the end of August, he launched the Pradhan Mantri Jan Dhan Yojana (PMJDY) for financial inclusion to extend bank accounts to every Indian household. Early last month, he was in Japan engaging with his counterpart, PM Shinzo Abe, promising a special fast track for all Japanese investors, playing *jugalbandhi* on drums and generally deepening the Indo-Japanese partnership. Back in India, the PM delivered a exhortatory Teacher's Day speech to millions of teachers and students. He then hosted Australia's Prime Minister Abbot and finalised an agreement to import uranium for India's nuclear programme. Within days, he was off to flood-ravaged Jammu and Kashmir to review the devastation and promise full support for reconstruction and rehabilitation. By mid-month, Modi was welcoming President Xi Jinping of China in Ahmedabad and Delhi, holding summit talks against the tense background of an untimely military standoff on the border and emphasising the importance of delineating the Line of Actual Control and solving the long-standing boundary issue.

24 September saw the PM in Bangalore at Indian Space Research Organisation's (ISRO) Tracking and Command Centre watching and celebrating the successful placement of India's Mars Orbiter in stable orbit around the red planet. The next day, he was back in Delhi launching the 'Make in India' programme in front of a galaxy of applauding industrialists. Then on to the United States (US), where he gave a strong speech at the United Nations General Assembly, wished the power of "The Force" to Hugh Jackman at an event in New York's Central Park, thrilled the packed non-resident Indian audience at Madison Square Garden, and had a small private dinner with

President Obama in Washington, followed by official talks the next day, which breathed new life into the flagging US-India relationship. Back in India, he launched the 'Swachh Bharat' programme on Gandhi Jayanti, celebrated Dussehra and then, over last weekend, kicked off Bharatiya Janata Party's (BJP) election campaign in the Maharashtra and Haryana assembly elections with a series of rousing speeches in both states. Like the legendary Superman, Narendra Modi seemed to be everywhere at the same time.

This whirlwind of media-intensive activity, oratory and multiple summitry had several positive consequences. It stamped the full authority of the PM on the government, after a long decade of weak and divided leadership under the United Progressive Alliance (UPA). It left all our major foreign interlocutors in no doubt as to who was in charge of the country. It amplified the sense of forward movement to most arms of the government. And, like his election campaign of earlier months, it fanned the hopes and aspirations of citizens and voters. All this was helped by the fact that Modi's high profile public speeches and press statements generally struck the right notes on all the varied range of subjects and audiences he took on.

The hyperactivity of the last few weeks also raises some important questions. Is there governmental capacity to deliver on all the promises that the PM has made to foreign and domestic audiences? For example, the PMJDY could become a very effective programme for financial inclusion, if it also becomes a game-changing vehicle for transforming India's massive, corruption-ridden and highly inefficient subsidies for food, fuel and fertiliser into much more efficient and targeted direct cash benefit transfers. Will this happen or might the PMJDY simply degenerate into one more expensive and inefficient populist give away of scarce public resources? How effectively can the central government take the Swachh Bharat programme forward, when its core elements of water, sanitation and waste disposal fall under the purview of state governments? Can a fast track favouring Japanese investments be made to work? How rapidly will the better business climate promised by PM to American corporate leaders actually fructify? Can the 'Make in India' boost to manufacturing take off without significant amendments to current laws on labour relations and land acquisition and major improvements in infrastructure sectors?

Besides the new promises of the past few weeks, what about the ongoing major economic and social challenges facing the nation, from old ones like stagnant employment, weak infrastructure, low economic growth and high inflation to new ones like the Supreme Court's retrospective cancellation of nearly all coal block allotments for captive mining? Behind these queries hangs another over-arching one: is this government too reliant on one man, the PM, or is there an effective team of ministers, officials and advisers in the making? A PM with energy, vision and commitment can certainly make a huge difference, but for sustained, successful governance of a nation of 1.25 billion people, he surely needs a competent and effective team? Is a strong Team Modi in the making?

A cursory review of our history over the past 40 years suggests that our most effective governments in taking the nation forward may have been the Narasimha Rao government of 1991-1996 and the Vajpayee government of 1998-2004. While these two governments obviously differed in many respects, they had three common ingredients which probably contributed significantly to their success. Both the governments were led by PMs with clear political authority, both had strong, competent ministers in cabinet and both had well-led and mandated set-ups in the PMO (prime minister's office).

Compared to these two examples, the political authority of Prime Minister Narendra Modi is clearly unquestionable and may indeed be stronger than that of either Rao or Vajpayee. However, Modi's ministerial team is composed mainly of newcomers to the Union government. As has been widely and frequently noted, competent and experienced ministers are few and look even fewer when the Minister for Finance, Defence and Company Affairs (Arun Jaitley) has to spend an entire month in hospital. Even with his fulltime return (for which we should all wish), the ministerial team is clearly weaker than Vajpayee's or Rao's. As a well-wisher of the government (indeed of any Government of India), I hope to see early appointment of two tried and tested stalwarts, Arun Shourie and Yashwant Sinha. They would add valuable competence, wisdom and heft to Team Modi.

At the PMO, Nripendra Misra is a fine, experienced and dedicated principal secretary. However, by all accounts, he does not start with the enormous advantages of either Amar Nath Varma or Brajesh Mishra in having his PM's confidence from the word go. One can only hope that this will be acquired and augmented over time.

Ultimately, the responsibility for creating and welding a strong and responsive Team Modi rests with the Prime Minister. The programmatic and political success of his government will depend substantially on the quality of his team of key ministers, officials and advisers.

09 October 2014.

28

Six Months On

In the coming fortnight, the Narendra Modi led National Democratic Alliance (NDA) government will complete six months in power, a good time for a preliminary stock-taking. What have been the notable economic and financial developments in these six months? What are the emerging policy priorities and initiatives of the new government? Are they well-crafted to deliver good results in terms of the objectives of strong, sustainable growth of output and employment, curbing inflation, alleviating poverty and strengthening India's external finances?

Before trying to answer these questions, it is important to recall the main features of the exceptionally weak economic legacy bequeathed by a decade of United Progressive Alliance (UPA) governance. This included: overall economic growth having collapsed to below 5 per cent for two successive years of 2012-13 and 2013-14, for the first time in a quarter century; industrial growth hovering near zero for over two years; employment stagnant; consumer inflation averaging 10 per cent for a record six years; external finances still vulnerable; major infrastructure sectors reeling from the backwash of massive scams in telecom and coal; public sector banks under serious stress; widespread policy paralysis and malfeasance across government ; and the heavy burden of populist legislation (such as for rural employment guarantee, food security and land acquisition). To use Finance Minister Arun Jaitley's oft-repeated understatement, the legacy was certainly 'challenging'!

Recent Economic Data

The official data that has emerged over the last six months is subject to three caveats: all data comes with a lag of typically one or two months; most of this data gets revised later; and finally, since policies influence economic outcomes with lags (variable and uncertain), much of the recently available information reflects, predominantly, the policies of the previous government. That said, here's what we know:

- Economic growth (in GDP [gross domestic product]) revived to 5.7 per cent in the first quarter of 2014-15, mainly because of an uptick in industrial production, exports and government-expenditure-driven services. Since all three elements have slowed in subsequent months and agriculture will be damped by the sub-par monsoon, GDP growth may well have slowed to 5 per cent or lower in the July-September quarter.

- Industrial growth (the focus of 'Make in India') rose to 4.2 per cent in the April-June quarter, but has subsided since, with all indications pointing to industrial production showing less than 2.0 per cent expansion in July-September 2014.

- Inflation, in consumer prices (CPI) is at last abating, from 10 per cent at the beginning of the calendar year to 6.5 per cent in September and looks well on track to meet the Reserve Bank of India's (RBI) target of below 6.0 per cent by January 2016. Policy factors (such as conservative monetary policy, restraint on food procurement prices and off-loading of excess public foodgrain stocks) have combined with good luck (the recent crash in international oil and other commodity prices) to bring about this healthy trend.

- External finances have improved; mainly because of sharply lower international oil and commodity prices and surging inflows of foreign portfolio investment into India's booming stock market. For medium-term strength, more rapid export growth remains necessary.

- Business expectations and stock markets have certainly soared since May, but such buoyancy has yet to reflect in indicators of real investment.

- The fiscal deficit of the Centre remains a worry, running at over 6.5 per cent of GDP in April-September 2014, mainly because of revenue shortfalls from exaggerated projections in the government's July Budget and despite the relief on subsidies from lower oil prices. Possible additional borrowing could put upward pressure on interest rates.

In short, the economic situation remains 'challenging'.

Economic Policy Initiatives

Both the July budget and subsequent developments have made plain this government's aversion to attempting 'big bang reforms' through legislative amendments to populist entitlement laws (rural employment, food security, education), the onerous new land acquisition act, the Indira Gandhi vintage, job-destroying central labour laws or even the notorious, retrospective "Vodafone amendment". However, since the disappointing July budget, clear signs of a pragmatic, incremental approach to policy improvements have emerged. Several strands of this broad strategy can be discerned and exemplified:

- Streamline, energise and improve governance and implementation. Examples include: the abolition of the numerous GOMs (Groups of Ministers) of dubious utility, the obvious strengthening of the PMO (Prime Minister's Office), dominated by a politically powerful and energetic PM; focusing on rapid resolution of governmental bottlenecks, such as environmental clearances, implementation of back-logged projects; and responding swiftly to fresh challenges, such as the Supreme Court's cancellation of coal block allocations.

- Rein in unsustainable fiscal populism. Here the examples include: the moderation of minimum support price increases for *kharif* crops to 2-3 per cent and limiting procurement from states which offer bonuses; raising of rail passenger fares by 15 per cent (after a decade of irresponsible non-adjustment); seizing the opportunity of lower international oil prices to deregulate diesel prices and cap cooking gas subsidy; and adjusting some parameters of the national rural employment guarantee scheme to reduce bogus claims and moderate expenditures.

- Push ahead with reforms where possible. These include: the diesel price deregulation; the enabling ordinance to conduct e-auction of coal blocks for designated uses, with a possibility of commercial mining; the renewed (and likely successful) push to obtain agreement with states on implementing the GST (goods and services tax); the raising of the foreign direct investment cap in defence industries to 49 per cent; and the path-breaking central government support (and consequential presidential assent) to the modest but significant labour law reforms by the Rajasthan government.

- Undertake social and economic mobilisation. Two prominent examples of this are the Swachh Bharat programme and the Pradhan Mantri Jan Dhan Yojana . The former commits long overdue political attention and capital to grave problems of basic cleanliness, sanitation and public health, although its programmatic and policy content remain to be defined. The latter, in concert with the reenergised Aadhar programme, could, potentially, transform India's massive, inefficient and corruption-ridden subsidy programmes into far more efficient direct cash benefit transfers.

Will Incrementalism Work?

That's the big question. As Zhou Enlai reportedly said about the success of the French Revolution, it's too early to tell. One has also to ask whether there really is an alternative? The so-called 'big bang' reforms of the early 1990s relied more on administrative measures (within the framework of extant legal authority) than on legislative changes. The latter are always more challenging for a government, especially when the ruling party is far short of a majority in the Rajya Sabha. One can also take hope from Minister Jaitley's recent reported statements that where legislative amendments are deemed essential (as perhaps in the case of the land acquisition act), they will be vigorously pursued.

My guess is that this multi-strand, incrementalist approach could achieve quite a lot. Economic growth may rise from 5.0-5.5

per cent this year to 6.0-6.5 per cent in 2015-16 and perhaps cross 7.0 per cent by 2016-17. But such improvement will not yield the pace of job creation that the 'youth bulge' requires. For that we need a more urgent and focused dismantling of constraints to labour-intensive manufacturing, whether they are labour laws, infrastructure deficiencies, foreign trade restrictions or skill shortages.

13 November 2014.

29

Politics, Priorities and Policies

It is all too easy for any government, especially a new Union government, to get caught up in the daily fire fighting of the myriad issues that arise in Parliament, media, foreign affairs, politics and administration. As Harold MacMillan, a justly famed British Prime Minister (PM) of the late-1950s and early-1960s, reportedly replied, when asked, what were the dominant policy themes of his prime minister-ship, "Events, dear boy, events!" In order to avoid this predicament in India's economic realm, it is important for the new Modi government to keep asking itself the question: what are the key economic policy goals the government has to pursue effectively to enhance its chances of re-election four and a half years from now. Based on past experience in India and other democracies, the answer seems pretty clear: more jobs, less inflation and better public services. Interestingly, if this troika of politically-inspired goals is successfully pursued, it is also likely to have satisfied most of the canons of good economic policy. Let me say a few words on the latter two goals, before turning to first objective of job growth.

Inflation

The rise in consumer prices at around 10 per cent a year over the six years 2008-2013 was a major factor behind the United Progressive Alliance (UPA) government's dismal electoral performance in the national elections of April-May 2014. The rate of increase has abated in the current year (down to 5.5% by October), thanks to a combination of policies, a fortuitous decline in international commodity prices and the persistence of weak economic activity. International commodity prices of oil, some metals and agricultural products are expected to stay soft for a year or two and are unlikely to repeat the 'super-cycle' of the past decade. The revival of domestic economic activity is likely to be gradual and should not spark another inflationary bout, provided our monetary and fiscal policies are kept prudent, increases in minimum support prices for agriculture are held moderate (as in the past year), excess public food-stocking is avoided and infrastructural bottlenecks are increasingly relieved. With these policies, and some good luck, inflation should not be a 'killer' in the next election.

Publicly Provided Goods and Services

The truth is that in our federal polity, the bulk of public services are provided by state and local governments. This is true of basic law and order, local roads, property records and transactions, water, sanitation and waste disposal (where available!), electricity distribution, primary and secondary education and health and so on. The big exceptions, where the central government plays a major role, include national highways, railways, tertiary education and health and, of course, the major subsidy-intensive schemes relating to public foodgrain distribution, fuel subsidies, fertiliser subsidies and rural employment guarantee.

In the coming years, the new government will have to work hard to revive the flagging national highway programme, vastly improve railway freight and passenger services and railway safety, as well as the quality and viability of tertiary education and health. Each of these is a major area requiring serious institutional and regulatory reform. But perhaps the biggest potential for reaping the economic and political dividends of good policy lies in reforming the mostly failing systems of major subsidies for foodgrains, fuel and fertiliser. The rapid expansion of the Aadhar footprint and the growing, countrywide penetration of bank accounts (recently accelerated by the Jan Dhan programme) offer the scope for transforming these hugely costly, badly targeted, leaky and corruption-ridden major subsidy schemes into much superior direct cash transfer systems. The experiment has already begun with cooking gas cylinders. Hopefully it will spread to kerosene, foodgrains and fertilisers soon. There will be sector-specific challenges in each, but surely worth overcoming.

Employment

Jobs! Jobs! Jobs! This, the biggest politico-economic challenge for the Modi government, is also the area in which timely, reliable data is scarcest. The latest National Sample Survey (NSS) (68th round) for employment is for 2011-12. It shows that India's labour force was nearly 500 million in January 2012, of which somewhere between 2.0 and 6.0 per cent were unemployed (depending on definition). Over half of this labour force was self-employed (exceeding 40% even in urban areas), less than a fifth (and less than a tenth in rural areas) were regular wage/salary employees and 30 per cent were casual labour. Although open unemployment was low, so were incomes, with regular wage employees averaging just under ₹400 per day and casual labour getting ₹170 in urban areas and ₹140 in rural areas (with females typically earning more than 30 per cent less than males). Since economic growth in the past three years has been slow and industrial production stagnant, the rates of unemployment and underemployment are almost certainly higher today, with little or no improvement in wage rates. Demographic projections indicate that there are about 10 million new jobseekers each year in a context of slow employment growth and extreme scarcity of well-paid, regular jobs. The critical importance of rapid job growth is obvious.

Asian and global development experience underlines the essential role of high economic growth and especially rapid expansion of labour-intensive manufacturing and construction sectors in generating jobs. 'Make in India' is certainly the right motto. But to convert slogan to reality, we need:

- Significant amendments to the new land acquisition act.

- Urgent broadening and deepening of the recent Rajasthan labour law reforms to the national level.

  (These two key reforms entail reversal of hugely anti-development and anti-employment bequests of the Gandhi ladies, Indira and Sonia).

- More effective and market-responsive programmes for skill development.

- Fixing the big infrastructure bottlenecks, especially in energy and transportation.

- Speedy roll-out of the GST (goods and services tax), to integrate India's market.

- Substantially greater transparency and stability in the tax and regulatory environment.

- Major improvements in the governance and performance of public sector banks (why not privatise a few?), and

- A well-managed, competitive exchange rate of the rupee.

Without rapid progress on this agenda, it is difficult to see how job growth can come anywhere near the requirements of the nation's aspiring jobseekers and this government's natural desire to get re-elected in 2019. To the extent political strength cannot be marshalled for effective reforms, it is to that extent the ruling party's chances of success in the hustling in future will decline.

---

13 November 2014.

30

Priorities for Budget 2015-16

The importance of Union Budgets for overall economic policy and outcomes is certainly high, but nowhere near the stratospheric levels to which the annual media hoopla typically sends it. This budget is, of course, more important than usual as it is anticipated by many as the 'first real budget' of the new Narendra Modi government, the July 2014 budget having been presented within six weeks of assuming office and having been deemed as something of a damp squib. In assessing any budget, I generally find it useful to focus on four distinct dimensions: the overall fiscal stance; the tax policies; the expenditure policies; and the vision-cum-reform elements. But before turning to priorities in each of these dimensions, let's take summary stock of the economic context for this budget.

Economic Context

The outlook for the world economy remains subdued, despite the steep drop in prices of oil and other commodities. The Chinese juggernaut is expected to slow further to below 7 per cent growth, Japan is unlikely to boom, and the stagnant European economy is burdened by legacy problems and the dark shadow of a Grexit from the eurozone. Only the United States (US) is recovering steadily, powered by years of expansionary fiscal and monetary policies, flexible and responsive markets and the revolution in shale oil and gas. Global growth in 2015 is likely to be a modest 2.5 per cent, with world trade expanding at an anaemic 2.0-4.0 per cent. Unpleasant surprises may lurk from Grexit, rebounding oil prices or a rise in US policy interest rates. So, the global economy may not be a force-multiplier for India's development in the year ahead.

Until end-January 2015, the well-accepted narrative for the Indian economy was clear: an economy slowly recovering from over two years of a serious growth slowdown, six years of double-digit inflation and a mini balance of payments crisis in 2013-14, with industry stagnant, infrastructure in disarray, stubborn fiscal deficits, weak government banks and stagnating employment. The re-based and revised national income estimates published on 30 January 2015 have created considerable confusion and debate by painting a more optimistic picture of growth in GDP (gross domestic product), industry and trade in 2013-14 than can be squared with the ground realities of an external finance crisis, high interest rates, slowing bank credit and tax revenues and sluggish corporate sales and earnings. Whatever the outcome of this debate, the 2015-16 Budget has to strive for faster growth of national output and employment, while nurturing lower inflation and sustainable external balance.

Overall Fiscal Stance

Although the Finance Ministry's *Mid-year Review* in December 2014 favoured a boost in public investment to spur growth, even at the expense of breaching the announced fiscal consolidation path, this may be unwise in the context of a weak and uncertain global economic environment. There is certainly a good case for raising public investment in roads, railways and ports, but this has to be accommodated within a prudent fiscal envelope. Given the recent, publicly reported commitments by the Prime Minister and the Finance Minister to peg the 2014-15 fiscal deficit at the budgeted level of 4.1 per cent of GDP, and bring it down to 3.0 per cent by 2016-17, the deficit level for 2015-16 has to be calibrated around 3.5-3.7 per cent of GDP. This modest reduction in the deficit (net government borrowing) will also support a sustained, growth-supportive reduction in nominal and real interest rates that has recently begun.

Tax Policies

It is important to recall that the Centre's gross tax receipts as a per cent of GDP had risen steadily from 8.0 per cent in 2001-02 to 12.0 per cent in 2007-08 (a major contributor to the improvement in public savings in this period), before declining thereafter. In 2014-15, it is expected to be below 10.0 per cent. In order to accommodate higher public investment and the (rumoured) increase in tax devolution to states recommended by the 14th Finance Commission, and ensure a modest reduction in the fiscal deficit, it is imperative to raise the gross tax revenues to GDP ratio significantly in 2015-16. Moreover, this projected increase has to be based on credible measures, not on absurdly optimistic revenue projections, as in 2013-14 and 2014-15, which then lead to hugely disruptive expenditure cuts. The six best ways of enhancing tax revenues in a credible and economically sensible way are:

- Increase the general rate of CENVAT (central value added tax) from 12 to 13 or 14 per cent; the latter was the rate before the 'global financial crisis'.

- A corresponding increase in the current rate of Services tax from 12.0 to 13.0 or 14.0 per cent.

- Drastically prune the myriad end-use, concessional rates and special exemptions currently embedded in both the Excise and Customs duty structures. This will yield considerable revenue, reduce economic distortions and special favours and pave the way to ushering in the GST (goods and services tax) in a year or two.

- Restoration of the customs duty on crude oil to 5.0 per cent.

- Increase special excises on luxury consumption goods such as cars and SUVs with higher (above 1600cc?) engine size, refrigerators above a threshold capacity, air-conditioners above a designated capacity, televisions above 36-inch screen size, and so forth. By confining such special excises (over and above the general CENVAT rate) to final consumption products, distortive consequences for the product chain will be avoided.

- Increase the cess on petrol and diesel, earmarked for roads by one per cent or so.

Also, avoid hair-brained proposals, such as to tax financial transactions and 'fringe benefits'. They have been tried before and failed.

Expenditures

On the expenditure side, in line with the recommendations of the Expenditure Commission's preliminary report (as indicated in the media) and the Shanta Kumar High Level Committee Report on the Food Corporation of India (FCI), the budget should announce road maps for direct cash transfer approaches in respect of existing major subsidies for kerosene, foodgrains and fertilisers, as has already been initiated for cooking gas cylinders. This will greatly enhance targeting of subsidies (currently there are huge leakages and corruption), while helping to contain their size.

Furthermore, with the funds from additional taxation and subsidy containment, the budget should ensure significantly higher expenditures for roads, ports, electricity transmission, public health and defence.

Reforms

Road maps for shifting major central subsidies to direct cash transfer approaches will constitute major reforms for the relevant sectors of petroleum, food and fertilisers. So will rapid progress on the implementation of the national GST. In addition, it would be very good if the budget announced:

- A roadmap for reform/restructuring and recapitalisation of public sector banks, which have huge value locked in their extensive networks but suffer from poor performance.

- A plan for reviving a credible approach to PPPs (private-public partnerships), which have run into all sorts of trouble in recent years.

- A roadmap on reform of labour laws, with the objective of encouraging much greater employment of India's growing population of young jobseekers.

These are my budget priorities and hopes. In a couple of weeks, it will be interesting to see to what extent, if any, these hopes are realised.

---

12 February 2015.

31

Budget 2015-16:
Above Average

On 28 February 2015, I was sitting in a TV studio, listening to the Finance Minister's budget speech and then offering early assessments along with other members of the 'expert panel'. Most of my fellow panellists rated the budget as 'excellent'. Despite feeling like an outcast, I could only muster an 'above average' rating. A dozen days later, the accumulation of commentaries on the budget suggest that much of the early euphoria has worn off and my initial assessment seem much less of an outlier and more in the mainstream. In any case, here are the reasons for my relatively restrained assessment, organised along my usual four fold framework.

Overall Fiscal Stance

Despite previous commitments to bring the fiscal deficit down to 3.6 per cent of GDP in 2015-16, the Finance Minister pressed the pause button on fiscal consolidation and targeted a marginal reduction down to 3.9 per cent of GDP from the 4.1 per cent reported for 2014-15 in the Revised Estimates (RE). Could he have done better? Yes, definitely, by raising more tax revenues by, for instance, increasing the general CENVAT excise rate to 13 per cent and restoring the modest customs duty of 5 per cent on crude oil imports, as well as by reducing further the central funding for state plans in line with Finance Commission recommendations.

More interestingly, should he have reduced the deficit further in the current and prospective economic/fiscal scenario? Yes again. Two of the reasons the Finance Minister gave for going slow with fiscal consolidation in 2015-16, namely uncertainty about GST implementation and the anticipated burden of the 7th Pay Commission Report, actually apply in 2016-17 and beyond, rather than in the coming year. Indeed, for precisely these reasons, it would have been better to undertake more deficit reduction in 2015-16 and less in the following two years. That is the exact opposite of the path chosen and raises significant doubts about the credibility of the announced consolidation trajectory.

Expenditure Policies

The budget has done a reasonably good job of accommodating the major restructuring of central government transfers to states mandated by the 14th Finance Commission. Its increased investment support to infrastructure sectors (especially railways and roads) by ₹70,000 crores, or 0.5 per cent of GDP (gross domestic product), is also most welcome. However, the overall increase in budgetary capital expenditure is a very modest 0.2 per cent of GDP, from 1.5 per cent of GDP to 1.7 per cent. That is disappointing.

Revenue expenditures on the other hand have come down by 0.9 per cent of GDP, from 11.8 per cent to 10.9 per cent. Two main factors have been at work: the reduction in transfers to support state plans and the 0.4 per cent of GDP reduction in major central subsidies. However, most of the latter reflects the good luck of sharply declining international oil prices, not significant policy reforms. Although the Minister's speech indicates the potential of JAM (Jan Dhan, Aadhar and mobiles) for better targeting and reduction of massive existing 'leakages' in subsidy programmes, there is no specific mention of extending this mechanism to the existing major subsidies for food, fertilisers and kerosene. Nor is there any reference to either the recent Shanta Kumar Committee report on restructuring foodgrain procurement, stocking and distribution or the Expenditure Commission's interim report, both of which favour phased implementation of direct cash benefit transfers for major subsidies. Does this presage a go-slow on such reforms in the backwash of the Delhi state election debacle?

Revenue Policies

Last month (*Business Standard*, 12 February), I had emphasised the importance of raising the Centre's gross tax revenue to GDP ratio, which had slumped from its peak of nearly 12 per cent of GDP in 2007-08 to below 10 per cent in 2014-15. This budget plans for a modest but welcome increase to 10.3 per cent of GDP from 9.9 per cent in 2014-15 (RE). However, this increase is predicated on the accuracy of the revenue projections. The 16 per cent increase projected in gross tax revenues seems a little optimistic, especially the 18 per cent increase in income tax revenue, when nominal GDP is expected to rise by only 11.5 per cent and given the significantly enhanced allowances and exemptions announced in the budget.

Mr Jaitley's strong backing for ushering in the national GST (goods and services tax) by April 2016 is commendable. However, daunting challenges remain, including passing the Constitution Amending Bill by a two-third majority in both houses of Parliament and getting approval of at least half the state legislatures. Moreover, the precise design elements relating to rate structure, exemptions, technology systems, etc., remain to be finalised and the chances of all this happening satisfactorily within a year are slim.

The budget also promises a significant reduction in the basic corporate tax rate from 30 per cent to 25 per cent over four years, with a concomitant reduction in the plethora of existing exemptions, to promote investment, growth and jobs. However this announcement of phased reduction would have had greater credibility and impact if there had been some actual reduction of the tax rate (and associated exemption pruning) in the coming year. None was forthcoming. Instead, the surcharge was increased from 10 per cent to 12 per cent!

As for non-tax revenues, the 2015-16 Budget continues to rely heavily on receipts from telecom spectrum auctions (about ₹40,000 crores) and disinvestment (nearly ₹70,000 crores). The first is not repeatable each year and the second has suffered from perennial shortfalls in execution, raising real issues of credibility for the fiscal deficit targets next year and beyond.

Broader Policy Initiatives

Mr Arun Jaitley's first full year budget is rich in broader policy announcements, encompassing schemes to strengthen insurance and social security for poorer segments of the population, steps to monetise gold stocks, measures to promote infrastructure investment, new laws against black money and steps to strengthen the policy framework for conducting economic and financial activity, including the ease of doing business. The formidable legislative agenda in the last category includes: a comprehensive new Bankruptcy Code, a new law on public procurement, a law for resolving disputes in public contracts, the merger of the Forward Markets Commission into the Securities and Exchange Board of India (SEBI), a new regulatory reform law to harmonise approaches across different infrastructure sectors, a new Indian Financial Code, an amendment to the Securitisation and Reconstruction of Financial Assets and Enforcement of Security Interest (SARFESI) Act to empower larger NBFCs (non-banking financial companies) and an amendment of the Reserve Bank of India (RBI) Act to establish a new Monetary Policy Committee to operationalise the new Monetary Policy Framework Agreement with RBI.

Most of these legislative initiatives are commendable in principle, although one has to suspend final judgment until the draft laws become available. For example, the proposed bill against black money 'stashed' abroad certainly appears draconian and runs the risk of vastly expanding the scope for extortionate behaviour by enforcement agencies. It might also discourage much legitimate and gainful cross-border financial and trade flows. Overall, the agenda is certainly challenging, although notable by their absence are initiatives to improve the governance and performance of public sector banks or to reform of our thicket of job-destroying labour laws.

Yes, an above average budget; how far above will depend on execution.

---

12 March 2015.

32

How Fast is India Growing?

How fast is the Indian economy growing? What is the sectoral composition or structure of the economy? How fast are major sectors expanding? Until two months ago, we thought we had a pretty good idea. Not so after 30 January 2015 when the Central Statistical Organisation (CSO) released its newly based estimates of national income and growth. Changes in base year are normal, and happen every seven or eight years to accommodate fresh data sources and changes in economic structure and methodological improvements. But this time (unlike ever before), the results of the base change, from 2004-05 to 2011-12, have led to substantial bemusement, bordering on incredulity, among many economists and analysts, including many in government and the Reserve Bank of India (RBI). What are some of the key issues and questions? Before we get into these, it is important to emphasise one point: there is no evidence of any of political agenda behind this puzzling exercise. Government and central bank officials seem as surprised and perplexed as those outside. It's a strictly 'made-in-CSO' conundrum.

Economic Growth

The growth story of the past dozen years, as per the old (2004-2005) base, is well-known: the unprecedented 9 per cent per year boom of 2003-04 to 2007-08, a dip below 7 per cent in 2008-09 following the global financial crisis and associated global recession, a smart recovery in 2009-10 and 2010-11, followed by a steep slowdown from 2011-12 onwards, yielding two successive years of below 5 per cent growth in 2012-13 and 2013-14, for the first time in 25 years. As the table shows, the new data tell a very different story for the three most recent years, the only three for which CSO has given estimates according to the new 2011-12 base. Yes, 2012-13 growth is still below

5 per cent, but then there is a surprising rebound to 6.6 per cent in 2013-14 (6.9 per cent as measured by GDP [gross domestic product] in market prices) and a further acceleration to 7.5 per cent in 2014-15 according to the 'advance estimates'.

It is these last two years, 2013-14 and 2014-15 (averaging 7 per cent growth according to the new base), which do not square with all the other available indicators: almost no industrial expansion according to the Index of Industrial Production or IIP (also produced by the CSO!); sluggish growth in tax revenues; lacklustre corporate earnings; slowing bank credit expansion (down to its lowest level in 21 years in 2014-15); slowing investment and exports; a weak employment market;...and so on. A growth rebound in 2013-14 is particularly puzzling, since that was the year when India experienced a mini BoP (balance of payments) crisis (with significant outflows of capital) and a 300 basis point policy interest rate hike during the second quarter. To my knowledge, nowhere else have such unpleasant events spurred significant economic recovery!

Sectoral Composition and Growth

The first two columns of the table compare the shares of some major sectors in GDP according to the two bases. Here are some noteworthy points:

- For years, policymakers and analysts have bemoaned the low share of manufacturing in India's GDP, below 15.0 per cent according to the familiar 2004-05 base. The new base tells us that the problem is perhaps not quite that bad, since it gives a share of 18.0 per cent. Apparently, this change is mainly due to sourcing industrial data from the Ministry of Corporate Affairs database on some 5 lakh company accounts (the MCA-21 data) for the first time. This may well be an improvement on past practice. The problem is that a non-official member of the relevant CSO sub-committee, Prof R. Nagaraj, has just published an article in the latest (28 March 2015) issue of the respected *Economic and Political Weekly,* raising serious issues with the manner in which CSO has used this data.

- Owing mainly to the availability of new sample data for 2010-2011, collected by the National Sample Survey (NSS), the estimated share of wholesale and retail trade (and hotels and restaurants) has declined sharply from over 17 per cent of GDP as per the old base to 11 per cent in the new base.
- On the other hand, the share of 'Finance, Real Estate and Business Services' in GDP has risen in the new base by a couple of percentage points to 19 per cent.

The new data also shows remarkably higher growth rates for two key sectors, manufacturing and trade/hotels/restaurants, in recent years, as compared to the estimates according to the 2004-05 base (see table). Thus, manufacturing is shown to be growing at 5.0-7.0 per cent in period 2012-2015, a good 4.0-6.0 per cent higher than estimated previously. As in the case of overall GDP, such robust rates of growth sit awkwardly with trends in all other known indicators such as tax receipts, bank credit, IIP, corporate earnings, employment, etc. Is this because of infirmities in the use of MCA-21 data?

The same uncomfortable disparities arise with the trade/hotels/restaurants sector. According to the old base, this sector barely managed one per cent growth in 2013-14. In contrast, the new base has it growing at above 13 per cent in the same year!

One could go on with raising more issues and puzzles. The real issue is what is to be done?

The Way Forward

It is clear that the new estimates of national income and growth do not readily pass the 'smell test'. Before they become the foundation of analytical descriptions and projections of the current, past and future trends in the Indian economy, a few things have to be done (most of which should have been done before publication of the new data series). Most importantly, the new methodology and the numbers it has yielded need to be subject to serious, independent, professional scrutiny. It is understood that the National Statistical Commission has been entrusted with such a review. That is certainly an important start. Second, before the Commission delivers its report (assuming it has been tasked to prepare one), it should organise one or more conferences of independent professional statisticians and economists on the matter. Third, before any further publication of any revisions to the latest data, it might be wise to compile the 'back series' (for at least 10-15 years) according to the new methodology. All this will entail hard work and discomfort for all concerned. But surely it is necessary and worthwhile to restore credibility to India's national income and growth estimates.

Until such review and revision is complete, we really can't be too sure about India's current, past and prospective growth rates. My own circumspect answer to the question in the title is that if India's GDP grew at around 5.5 per cent in 2014-15 according to the old base, it will probably register 6.0 per cent plus growth in 2015-16 according to the same yardstick. Not stellar, but better than nearly all other large economies in today's world.

Table 32.1

Changes in Growth and Sectoral Shares of GDP (GVA)

Shares (%) in Current Prices			Growth at Constant Prices					
(Average of 2011-12 and 2012-13)		*Major Sectors*	*2012-13*		*2013 -14*		*2014-15*	
2004-05 Base	*2011-12 Base*		*2004-05 Base*	*2011-12 Base*	*2004-05 Base*	*2011-12 Base*	*2004-05 Base*	*2011-12 Base*
17.7	18.2	Agriculture/Forestry/Fishing	1.4	1.2	4.7	3.7	3.5	1.1
14.4	18.0	Manufacturing	1.1	6.2	-0.7	5.3	1.8	6.8
17.3	11.1	Trade/Hotels/Restaurants	4.5	10.3	1.0	13.3	3.3**	8.4**
16.9	19.2	Finance/Real Estate/Business Services	10.9	8.8	12.9	7.9	10.0	13.7
100.0	100.0	Total GDP (GVA)	4.5	4.9	4.7	6.6	5.5	7.5

Notes: * Data in this column are growth rates for first half of 2014-15; second half not published on 2004-05 base.

** Data refer to wider sector, including Transport and Communications.

Sources: Ministry of Statistics and Programme Implementation Press Notes of 28 November 2014, 30 January 2015 and 9 February 2015.

2011-12 base data refer to Gross Value Added (GVA) at "Basic Prices", while 2004-05 base data refer to GDP at factor cost. These concepts are almost equivalent.

09 April 2015.

33

On Balance, a Good Year

In less than a fortnight, the National Democratic Alliance (NDA) government led by Narendra Modi will complete its first year in office. The flood of assessments in newspapers and other media has already begun. Here is my tuppence worth, limited strictly to the economic domain.

First, an important methodological point. Much of what one reads offer judgements based on comparing the values of key economic outcome variables (such as economic growth, inflation, fiscal deficits, external imbalances, currency levels, sectoral performance indicators, etc.) for the most recent year, 2014-15, with the previous one or more years. This is too simplistic and misleading. The performance of the Indian economy in 2014-15 was dependent on many factors, including, notably: the initial (inherited) conditions, the influence of past policies, exogenous factors (such as commodity price falls, rainfall deficiencies, global economic weaknesses) and last (and perhaps the least!), the fresh initiatives launched by the new government. Thus, it is well known that the NDA government inherited a pretty awful economic situation in terms of the usual metrics of growth, inflation, external imbalances, stagnant employment, infrastructure disarray, etc., as well as the backwash of massive scams in telecom and coal, serious stresses in public sector banks, widespread policy paralysis across government, the lasting burden of ill-designed, populist legislation, and long-pending structural problems in urbanisation, environment, labour and land markets. Whichever government had come to power in May 2014 would have been seriously challenged to improve economic performance in the short run.

Therefore, the better way to assess the new government's economic record is to focus on its policy initiatives during the year. In particular, let us focus on those policy initiatives which: (a) reduce consumer price inflation (I, for short), (b) enhance the provision of central government services (S) and, above all, (c) revive the momentum of growth, investment and employment (GIE). If these are wide-ranging, well-designed and effective, the likelihood of sustained, good economic performance outcomes will be high.

The Modi government's array of first-year economic policy initiatives has been impressive and broadly sensible. They include:

- Reasonable fiscal moderation, including through abolition of the subsidy on diesel and a capping of the subsidy on cooking gas (I).

- Successful inflation control through deployment of excess public food stocks, scaled back increments in procurement prices, conservative monetary policy and the good luck of plunging international commodity prices (I).

- Significant thrust to railway investment, efficiency and financial viability (including the first increase in passenger fares in a decade), although this is clearly a work in progress (S).

- Some advance in reviving the flagging programme for national highways (S).

- Major acceleration (through the Jan Dhan Yojana) in expanding the spread of household bank accounts nation-wide (S).

- Using this expanded bank platform to offer low-end life and accident insurance, and a contributory pension scheme for unorganised workers (S).

- Sustained and ongoing efforts to constructively amend the unworkable new land acquisition act passed by the previous government in 2013 (GIE).

- Providing the necessary support to the Rajasthan (and later Haryana) government's successful initiatives to reform existing labour laws in order to promote more and better jobs (GIE).

- Amendment of the Apprenticeship Act, reducing the labour laws, 'inspector *raj*' and moving towards online compliance (GIE).

- Initiation of the plan to integrate three key labour laws (the Industrial Disputes Act, the Trade Unions Act and the Industrial Employment [Standing Orders] Act) into a single, job-promoting industrial labour code (GIE).

- Determined and ongoing efforts to bring the game-changing, nation-wide GST (goods and services tax) into being by April 2016 (GIE).

- Broadly successful conclusion of the Supreme Court mandated auction of coal blocks, after enacting the necessary legislative amendment (GIE).

- Amendment of the old Mines and Minerals (Regulation and Development) Act to enable auctioning of licenses and establishment of a National Minerals Exploration Trust to explore and promote non-coal minerals (GIE).

- Completing the long-pending amendment of insurance legislation to lift the cap on foreign ownership from 26 per cent to 49 per cent (GIE).

- Raising the foreign ownership cap in defence industries to 49 per cent as part of serious effort to open up defence production to domestic and foreign firms (GIE).

However, there have also been lacunae and disappointments relating to the government's first year policy programme. These include:

- A hesitant approach to rationalising some of massive, ill-targeted and corruption-ridden subsidies that plague India's economy. The two biggest ones now are for food and fertilisers, each amounting to about one lakh crore (inclusive of arrears). This, despite the government's own reports (notably the Shanta Kumar report and the Expenditure Commission reports) favouring a phased transition towards direct cash transfers in these areas, especially given the technical feasibility provided by the "J-A-M" combination of the Jan Dhan Yojana, Aadhar and mobiles. The money saved from such rationalisation could be very fruitfully used to expand irrigation and other rural infrastructure (S, GIE).

- A willingness to tolerate the rupee's over valuation, to the detriment of both exports and import-competing domestic industry (GIE).

- Inaction, thus far, on the Shanta Kumar Committee report's recommendations for broader reform of the food economy (GIE).

- Lack of a clear roadmap to deal with serious problems of balance sheet weakness, governance and performance of public sector banks, coupled with a reluctance to reduce a majority of government ownership (GIE).

- Little discernible progress in redesigning the faltering approach of PPP (private-public partnerships) in executing infrastructure (GIE);

- Avoidable errors in tax policy and administration, such as the recent flip-flop on the application of MAT (minimum alternate tax) to foreign portfolio investors (GIE).

- The draconian new bill against black money abroad, which may discourage legitimate economic transactions and increase the scope for harassment by enforcement agencies.

- A rising concern that an increasingly centralised system of decision-making, with a strong Prime Minister's Office (PMO), may be encouraging a new kind of 'policy paralysis', where line ministries hesitate to take autonomous administrative decisions without seeking approval from PMO.

On balance, the Modi government's first year of economic policy initiatives has been good, certainly better than any of the last 10 years under the previous government. Quite a few of these initiatives are still 'work in progress', battling constraints imposed by parliamentary politics, legacy problems or administrative/technical limitations. Hence their impact, and even of the 'enacted initiatives', on future outcome economic variables will take time to bear fruit. The broad direction of policy is clearly sound. The scale and timing of the yield in terms of higher growth, more employment, lower inflation and better services is, inevitably (and uncomfortably), uncertain and subject to the vagaries of weather, global conditions and the broader political dynamics.

---

14 May 2015.

Burden of Legacies

As monsoon showers blanket the country, the prevailing economic mood is still one of waiting for the economic recovery. Few pay heed to the controversial, new series GDP (gross domestic product) growth data, which indicate that the recovery began (improbably) in 2013-14 and is now in full swing. All the other indicators (index of industrial production, purchasing managers' indices for manufacturing and services, bank credit growth, corporate earnings and tax revenue growth) still suggest a sluggish economy, marking time and struggling to rebound. There are conflicting signs on the investment cycle, certainly nothing to suggest a full-blooded recovery. If one steps back from the present, and looks at the various legacy constraints and impediments to a vigorous revival, the current situation is hardly surprising. Some of these legacy constraints go back several decades; others are due to fresh policy mistakes of the last 10 years. Here I list my "top 10", six from the earlier past and four from the latest decade of United Progressive Alliance (UPA) governance.

Enduring Hold of Old Legacies

a) Subsidies for electricity, irrigation water and fertilisers to agriculture: Half a century ago, when agriculture (mostly small farmer) accounted for over half of GDP and three-quarter of total employment, it may have been sensible to subsidise these inputs to catalyse the spread of modern agricultural practices. By the late 1980s, professional opinion had shifted in favour of replacing these burgeoning subsidies with investment in modern transport networks, medium and minor irrigation and other rural infrastructure. Unfortunately, the path dependence of politics ensured that the subsidies stayed, although state electricity boards went bankrupt (today they owe suppliers and banks around ₹300,000 crore!), water tables plummeted, costly irrigation command areas remained woefully under-utilised, and overuse of urea damaged soil fertility.

b) Nationalised Banks: Forty-five years ago, Indira Gandhi nationalised the major private banks as part of the *garibi hatao* campaign, which assured her victory over the Congress old guard. Bank nationalisation did little to alleviate poverty, even though it did accelerate the pace of branch expansion. It also spawned bureaucratic cultures, widespread behest lending, pervasive inefficiency and frequent need for budgetary recapitalisation. Despite 25 years of financial sector reform, government-owned banks continue to dominate Indian banking and are plagued by weak governance, low capitalisation, serious operational inefficiencies and, in recent years, worryingly vulnerable balance sheets.

c) Labour Laws: Indira Gandhi's severe tightening of labour laws in the emergency year 1976, notably through the insertion of the highly restrictive chapter V(B) in the Industrial Disputes Act (further tightened in 1982), has hugely discouraged fresh employment in the organised sector, constraining its share in total employment to around 10-15 per cent, far below levels in comparable economies like China and Indonesia. These exceptionally restrictive laws have also stunted the development of medium and large scale, labour-intensive manufacturing, thus undermining the most potent transmission belt between growth and employment generation. Fortunately, the new Narendra Modi government has begun a decades-overdue process of reforming these laws.

d) Neglect of Urban Governance: The Constitution of India, framed 65 years ago, did not find a place for 'third tier', local government institutions in either urban or local areas. As a result, the planning, execution and governance of urban land use and key services such as transport, water supply, sanitation and waste disposal remained woefully inadequate, despite the gathering pace of urbanisation. Some improvement occurred in 1992 through the 73rd and 74th amendments to the Constitution, mandating some powers for local rural and urban bodies, respectively. But it was far from enough. Little wonder that most Indian cities and towns are today such messy, under-serviced semi-slums, constraining the rapid development of non-agricultural activities. The visions of smart cities, bullet trains and civic cleanliness are fine, but their actuation will require serious and rapid empowerment of ULBs (urban local bodies).

e) Unreformed Administrative Structures: Independent India inherited a colonial civil service system focused on collecting revenue and maintaining law and order among the 'natives'. In the nearly 70 years that have elapsed since then, there have been several administrative reforms commissions offering tomes of recommendations for necessary change, including, most recently, during the decade-long tenure of the Gandhi-Singh led UPA government. But change has been slow in coming, far slower than in the 'parent' civil service in Britain, which long ago reformed its structure to better incorporate the specialist needs of effective modern governance. Caste-based reservations have compounded the problems. Little wonder that Indian bureaucracy has gained notoriety in blocking development and change and has had limited success in deploying sector-specific expertise effectively. However, nearly seven decades of experience offer little hope for serious reform.

f) Neglect of Public Health: It is well known that people of India suffer from terrible health: around 40 per cent of all children under 3 years are stunted, over half of all married women (aged 15-49) are anaemic, communicable diseases are rampant and all this extracts an enormous economic toll from both individuals (especially the poor) and the nation's economy. Much of this huge loss is avoidable by directing greater focus on preventive public health services (including better water and sanitation), an area which has received scant attention (outside Tamil Nadu and perhaps Kerala), as compared to vaccination programmes and curative medical services. Hopefully, the Modi government's emphasis on the 'Swachh Bharat' programme will help reverse this age-old, costly neglect.

New Legacies

The recent decade of UPA governance has added to the list of challenging legacies.

g) Land Acquisition Act (2013): This UPA legacy is a hot political issue. By most sober accounts, the new law is largely unworkable, even for land acquisition by public agencies for *bona fide* development needs. And for private firms it will raise land costs several fold, making many job-creating activities uneconomic. But much similar to our populist legislation, now that it is on the books, it is proving enormously difficult to amend in sensible ways. The Modi government is trying hard to make sensible, limited amendments. Failure will cost dearly in terms of the nation's economic expansion and job growth.

h) Entitlement Laws: During its tenure, the Gandhi-Singh government enacted three important entitlement-expanding laws relating to rural employment, food security and education. The goals are laudable. The problems lie with poor design and the basic issue of committing prematurely to open-ended fiscal obligations, without undertaking the concomitant task of widening the tax base. At present, the full impact (both good and bad) of these laws is moderated by non-fulfillment of certain necessary conditions at the state level. Once these are satisfied, the full costs of premature fiscal populism will emerge and are likely to be untenable.

i) Backwash of Major Scams: The massive scams during the UPA decade in telecom spectrum allocation, coal block allotment, illegal iron ore mining and so on are well known, as are the corrective actions through Supreme Court decisions and follow-up actions by the successor government. For the concerned sectors, the transitional economic costs have been huge and will take time to be absorbed. Additionally, the general principle of auctioning public economic resources has become widely accepted. While this will reduce large scale corruption, it may also blunt the competitive edge arising from access to cheap inputs.

j) Crony Capitalism: Crony capitalism is not new. What has been novel is the vigour with which it flourished during the past decade of high corporate growth, combined with exceptionally weak national governance. The new government has taken determined steps to rein in this unsavory phenomenon. But the nexuses run deep and wide, and the battle could be long and uncertain.

9 July 2015.

IV

General

35

Myanmar
India's Neglected Neighbour

Few people in India know that we share a border of over 1,600 km with Myanmar (aka Burma), comparable in length with our borders with Bangladesh, China and Pakistan. The latter three are very much part of our daily diet of news and discussion. Almost every Indian is an expert on Pakistan. There is no lack of Bangladesh analysts. And even the tribe of China watchers is on the rise. But Burma analysts in India? It's hard to find any outside a small group of serving and retired foreign service, intelligence and military officials. There may be good explanations for our collective absence of mind. But they cannot be justifications. The fast-moving changes in Myanmar in the last 15 months are throwing up important challenges and opportunities, which we cannot afford to neglect.

Until 1937, Burma was a part of British India and was linked quite closely with eastern India, especially Bengal. Many thousands of Indians (traders, professionals, workers) had made their home in Rangoon, Mandalay and other Burmese towns. The separation of Burma in 1937 ended unfettered Indian immigration. As the Japanese army swept across Burma in 1942, thousands of ethnic Indians fled across the mountains and jungles to Assam and Bengal. Thousands more left at Independence and "400,000 others were compelled to leave in 1964 after the ultra-nationalist army regime had come to power in 1962" (see Thant Myint-U's recent fine historical travelogue, *Where China Meets India*). General Ne Win's "Burmese way of socialism" from 1962-1988 turned Burma firmly inwards, severing most of the economic ties with the outside world, including India.

The tumultuous events of 1988 saw the meteoric rise of the charismatic Daw Aung San Suu Kyi as the leader of democratic forces. The student revolts were brutally suppressed by a new military regime, State Law and Order Restoration Council (SLORC), which abrogated the 1974 Constitution and formally imposed martial law. Suu Kyi was placed under house arrest in 1989, where she remained for over 15 of the next 21 years. Strangely, the regime went ahead with national elections in 1990, which were won overwhelmingly by Suu Kyi's National League for Democracy (NLD). SLORC ignored (and later annulled) the inconvenient results and tightened its grip over all aspects of political and economic life in Myanmar, especially after the ascent of Than Shwe as the ruling general in 1992. For the next 19 years, until his voluntary resignation in March 2011, Than Shwe ruled Myanmar as undisputed head of the State Peace and Development Council (SPDC), as SLORC was renamed in 1997.

The government of Rajiv Gandhi had initially supported the democratic movement quite strongly. But the exigencies of realpolitik soon asserted themselves. India needed Myanmar's cooperation to deal with insurgencies in her Northeast. And the surge in China's economic and political influence over Myanmar made reengagement with the military government increasingly urgent. By mid-1990s, such reengagement was fully under way. However the scale and pace of India's economic engagement with Myanmar remained modest compared with China's billions of dollars of infrastructure development (dams, roads, railways and oil/gas pipelines), trade and arms supplies and an estimated two million Chinese now living and working in north-central Myanmar, with a strong contingent in Mandalay.

Given the Myanmar's strategic location, the importance of stronger economic links between our Northeast and Myanmar, the enormous potential benefits of a land-link from the Northeast to the Bay of Bengal and the potential to expand bilateral trade and investment, our economic engagement has been inadequate. This was true even in 2010. Now, after the events of the last 15 months, there is an urgent need to accelerate implementation of major ongoing projects (such as Sittwe port and the Kaladan multi-modal transport link) and facilitate greater bilateral trade and investment.

What has happened in Myanmar recently? A great deal. First, although the election of November 2010 was carefully 'managed', with 25 per cent of the parliamentary seats reserved for the military and three-quarter of the remainder won by the ruling regime's Union Solidarity and Development Party (USDP), a Parliament now exists with over 15 per cent of opposition members (minus the NLD which could not contest). Second, for the first time in Myanmar's history there has been formal decentralisation of some executive and legislative powers to the 14 regions/states, with USDP in a minority in six of the seven ethnic state assemblies (although in a majority when combined with the 25.0% military reservation). Third, Aung San Suu Kyi was released a week after the election and has enjoyed increasing freedom (especially after March 2011) to speak, write, travel within Myanmar and meet visiting foreign dignitaries. Fourth, General Than Shwe resigned from the Presidency in March 2011 and ensured succession by U Thein Sein, Prime Minister since 2007, the principal architect of the 2008 Constitution, the government's chief representative at international fora and deemed untainted by crony business connections unlike several other top military contenders for President.

Fifth, President Thein Sein has moved swiftly with reform measures, including: appointment of technocrats in several ministerial posts; loosening of censorship, release of several batches of political prisoners; a meeting and dinner with Daw Suu Kyi in Nay Pyi Taw in August 2011; re-registering of the hitherto banned NLD as a legitimate political party in November 2011; announcement of the April 2012 by-elections to 48 parliamentary seats; fresh initiatives towards peace accords with Myanmar's ethnic insurgents; shelving in September 2011 of the environmentally suspect, Chinese-sponsored $ 3.6 billion dam at Myitsone; and unusual willingness to engage with external governments. The last included his visit to India in October 2011, his current tour of some Association of South East Asian Nations (ASEAN) capitals and recent well-publicised visits to Myanmar by Hillary Clinton and other Western ministers as well as others including President Zardari of Pakistan. Such visits typically entailed dialogue with the government in Nay Pyi Taw and with Daw Suu Kyi in Yangon.

In response to these reform steps and wider geopolitical considerations the US has announced up-gradation of diplomatic relations to ambassadorial level and the European Union (EU) is proceeding with relaxation of visa restrictions against government members. Gradual relaxation of long-standing Western economic sanctions is also on the cards, conditional on further civil and political reforms. Last fortnight, in Delhi, foreign minister Maung Lwin publicly stated that the reform process was "irreversible". In a more nuanced remark, he characterised the reforms as "incremental, systematic and dynamic".

There have been false dawns in Myanmar before. But this looks like the real thing. A more pluralistic political system is clearly emerging, even if full-fledged democracy is not imminent. Myanmar's future is fundamentally in the hands of her people but friendly nations can help. India is unusually well-placed to assist, in the long-term interest of both nations. In the final pages of his book, U Thant's grandson sketches alternative futures for Myanmar. In the happier scenario, "In Burma, where China meets India, a unique meeting place of cultures and peoples is created, at this new centre of the Asian world. Progress in Burma would be a boon for the region. A peaceful prosperous and democratic Burma would be a game-changer for all Asia." Let us hope that this future prevails.

9 February 2012.

36

Myanmar's Economy
Some Glimpses

Sixty years ago, Myanmar (then Burma) was one of the economically better-off countries in Asia, with abundant and valuable resources of forests, gems and minerals, a major exporter of rice from the fertile Irrawaddy delta and an average income higher than nearly all Asian nations other than Japan. Today, after 50 years of military rule, with the first 25 under General Ne Win's "Burmese way of socialism", the relative rankings seem to have changed dramatically, with Myanmar having one of the lowest average incomes among Asian countries. How did this happen? What was the trajectory of growth and development that led to this unfortunate reversal of fortune? The truth is that we know very little.

If you go to the Asian Development Bank (ADB) website's country "Fact Sheet" on Myanmar, you can learn that around 2010, the population was 60 million growing at a relatively low 1.3 per cent per year, adult literacy was a high 92 per cent, urbanisation a middling 34 per cent and the poverty ratio (according to some undefined national poverty line) was 26 per cent. Interestingly, the Fact Sheet does not report a number for per capita national income. For that, you have to dig deeper in the brief chapter on Myanmar in the ADB's recent (April 2012) *Asian Development Outlook*. That reports a number of $715 for 2011, lower than for Bangladesh and Cambodia, about half Vietnam's and a little less than half of India's. Indeed, given that India's per capita GNP (gross national product) is more than double Myanmar's, it is interesting that the latter's urbanisation is a bit higher, poverty ratio lower and adult literacy much better. But beware the data, especially that of Myanmar.

The most recent economic assessment of Myanmar by an international institution is the International Monetary Fund's (IMF) 2011 Article IV Consultation report, completed in March 2012 and placed on the IMF website last month. The team that prepared the report included members from the World Bank and the ADB (. A striking feature of the report is the massive downward adjustment to the double-digit official GDP (gross domestic product) growth data carried out by the IMF team (see Table 35.1). This revision apparently has the government's concurrence as reported in the IMF report. The overestimation in official growth data is apparently due to excessive reliance on public sector indicators in an economy where 90.0 per cent of economic activity occurs in the private sector. It is one of many serious data gaps in Myanmar, which bedevil both historical and concurrent assessments of economic performance.

Table 35.1

Myanmar: Selected Economic Indicators

	2007-08	2008-09	2009-10	2010-11 (Est.)	2011-12 (Projected)	2012-13
Real GDP growth, official (%)	12.0	10.3	10.6	10.4	-	-
Real GDP growth IMF (%)	5.5	3.6	5.1	5.3	5.5	6.0
Consumer prices inflation (%)	32.9	22.5	8.2	8.2	4.2	5.8
Public sector deficit (% of GDP)	3.8	2.4	4.8	6.0	5.5	4.6
Current account balance (% of GDP)	0.4	-2.9	-2.7	-0.8	-2.7	-4.4
Foreign exchange reserves (months of total imports)	6.6	6.3	7.9	8.9	9.4	9.7
Exchange rate (parallel market, Kyat/$)	1,110	992	1004	861	810*	-

Note: *As of January, 2012.

Source: IMF Article IV Consultation Report, May 2012. See *www.imf.org*

The pervasive data problem is colourfully described in a recent (March 2012) public speech by Dr U Myint, the leading economic advisor to President Thein Sein and head of the Myanmar Development Research Institute. Myint likens the challenge of successful economic and social development to an automobile race, in which quality of the car proxies for sound economic policies. He paints Myanmar's past economic policies as an out dated car with a faulty instrument panel:

> Going back to the car again, it may be desirable to begin by fixing the dials, gauges and meters on the instrument panel that are not functioning properly. The speedometer looks particularly suspicious. We know from experience that a car of this vintage cannot be speeding along at the rate the speedometer seems to be showing. If it does, there is a danger of the engine overheating. Unfortunately, the thermostat has broken down so there is no device to warn us of this danger. In the meantime...the gas tank is empty and the car is running on its emergency fuel reserve. To add to our woes, the mileage indicator got stuck several years ago. So although we are aware the car is in motion, we are unsure of the direction it is heading, have no clear idea of the distance that has been covered, and are mostly in the dark as regards the miles we have to go...to reach the finish line. This is not a good situation for any participant in a race. Hence, fixing the dials and gauges and improving the quality and availability of our statistical indicators, data and information seems like one area that deserves priority attention at the present time.

There could hardly be a more persuasive plea for improving vastly the database for undertaking sound social and economic policies.

Unfortunately, policymaking cannot await the long overdue improvement of data systems. Fortunately, the initiatives in economic policy over the past year by the new civilian government seem to be broadly in the right direction. They include the moves towards an unified and broadly market-determined exchange rate (in April); presentation of a budget to Parliament, which uses higher revenues from gas sales to target a reduction of the public sector deficit; increased budget allocations for education and health and a lower one for military spending; enhanced authority to the central bank; and welcoming of foreign investment in energy and hydropower.

These moves are welcome but only a beginning. Significantly, greater resources have to be deployed for public education and health. The nascent manufacturing sector needs to be nurtured through supportive policies so that it grows to be a major job-generating sector in future. There is substantial potential as low-skill manufacturing activities relocate from China and other higher-wage East Asian neighbours. Agriculture and rural development require broad-based support from infrastructure, credit and other inputs as well as far-reaching reforms of land tenure.

In the meantime, Myanmar will have to contend with managing an inward capital surge in search of her rich resources, with Western nations having lifted various economic sanctions. The exchange rate has already appreciated significantly to the detriment of rice exports and could hurt tourism, which has enormous job-creating potential.

After several decades of sub-par performance, Myanmar has resumed the long journey of broad-based, economic and social development. That in itself is very welcome.

14 June 2012.

37

Gandhian Legacies

December is the month when columnists tend to offer their forecasts for the new year ahead or review the year gone by. I will do both but over a much longer time frame than a year. As I ponder over the wreckage of our growth and development aspirations in the past two years, I am struck by the path-dependence of our economic policies and performance. That is, our economic ideas, policy choices and consequences from 40 years ago continue to constrain and influence our policies and performance today. Hence, the reference to legacies in the title. Indira Gandhi's economic policies (1966-1984, with a 3-year Janata interregnum) still exert powerful, usually negative, effects on current economic performance and policies. Similarly, looking ahead, I would venture to suggest that the policy omissions and commissions of the Gandhi-Singh government since 2004 will continue to constrain our developmental trajectory in the years ahead. Let me illustrate.

Consider the following three Indira Gandhi economic policies, whose consequences are still prominent in the Indian economic landscape. The nationalisations of banking and insurance were carried out in 1969 and 1970, motivated by a combination of pro-poor 'socialist' ideology and hard-headed political calculus. More than 40 years later, despite liberalisations and reforms conducted over the past 20 years, 70.0 per cent of bank deposits lie with government-owned banks and the government-owned Life Insurance Corporation (LIC) remains the dominant firm in the industry. While bank nationalisation undoubtedly accelerated the spread of bank branches in India and curtailed the unhealthy nexus between industrial houses and some erstwhile private banks, it also spawned some of the well-known deficiencies of government banks. These included the rise of a bureaucratic/departmental culture in banking, the proliferation of lending at the behest of political masters, frequent need for recapitalisation at taxpayer expense, and growth of new kinds of unhealthy nexus between politicians, bankers and industrialists. Hardly any independent financial expert would defend the current prominence of public sector banks in India today on the grounds of economic efficiency and financial prudence. Yet it persists. The new vested interests, coupled with residual political ideology, have successfully stymied all efforts since the late 1990s to reduce government ownership below 51 per cent.

Second, in 1967 the policy of SSI (small scale industry) reservations was initiated (and strengthened in 1980). This shut out medium and large-scale Indian firms from precisely those labour-intensive, manufactured products (garments, shoes, toys, sporting goods, small electrical appliances, etc.) in which the East Asian tiger economies achieved their manufacturing-exports-led growth in the decades after 1970. It turned out that, as a general rule, the India's SSI units were too small and inefficient to realise the economies of scale and scope necessary to compete successfully in international markets. So, the SSI reservation policy seriously stunted the rise of an internationally competitive, labour-using manufacturing sector in India. Since the late 1990s, efforts to chip away gradually at this damaging, Gandhi-sponsored policy has met with success, but not before substantial harm had been inflicted on Indian industry's capacity for growth, exports and employment.

Perhaps the most damaging of Indira Gandhi's economic legacies was the severe tightening of labour laws carried out in the "Emergency year" of 1976 through the insertion of the restrictive chapter V(B) in the Industrial Disputes Act. In effect, this made it almost impossible for an industrial enterprise with more than 300 employees to either retrench its workforce or even close down, without government permission, which was rarely given. The law was tightened further by lowering the threshold level of employees to 100 in 1982. The provisions essentially turned labour from a variable factor of production into a fixed one! The massive discouragement to fresh employment ensured that India's organised sector employment (including 9 million government administrative employees) stagnated at less than 30 million out of a total labour force of around 500 million. In 2010, organised manufacturing accounted for less than 1.5 per cent of the nation's work force! In essence, such restrictive laws bought job security for a tiny fraction of the working class at the cost of condemning over 90.0 per cent of workers to casual/informal employment, with low earnings and negligible job security. By negating India's comparative advantage in labour-intensive manufacturing, these laws helped ensure that India's manufacturing sector stagnated at around 15.0-16.0 per cent of GDP (gross domestic product), compared to over 30.0 per cent in China. Labour laws and SSI reservation policy were important factors explaining the absence of a large and growing class of factory workers in India, in strong contrast to East Asian nations where this category formed the core of a rising middle class. Today, as China grows rich (with average income more than triple of that of India already), labour-intensive manufacturing is migrating to Vietnam, Cambodia and Bangladesh, but not India, where the employment crisis continues to build. The tragedy is that no major party supports labour law reform.

What might be some of the enduring new constraints on India's economic development bequeathed by the nine years (and counting) of the Gandhi-Singh United Progressive Alliance (UPA) government? First, the massive increase in subsidies, government wage-bill and entitlement programmes that occurred in 2008-09 converted a decent fiscal situation into a structural fiscal problem. Even by the government's understated accounting, the combined (centre and states) fiscal deficit jumped from 4.0 per cent of GDP in 2007-08 to 8.3 per cent in 2008-09, where it remained in 2011-12, with little prospect of any significant reduction this year or next. The costs in terms of higher inflation, higher interest rates, lower investment and growth and larger external deficits are likely to continue a good deal longer. Second, prolonged, weak, diarchic governance has taken its toll on an already stressed government administrative machinery in ways that may be long-lasting, to the detriment of public policy. Weak governance has also allowed the proliferation of massive scams (such as in telecom, coal mining and land allocation), which have taken crony capitalism to new heights (or is it lows?) in India. Quite apart from the damage to the specific sectors, the tolerance of such nexuses for so long may have encouraged a persistent pattern of undesirable linkages between politicians, bureaucrats and business. Third, the greatly heightened dependence on imported energy and raw materials and a pattern of large external deficits have undoubtedly increased India's vulnerability and reduced her economic security in ways that will challenge policymakers in the years ahead. Finally, and perhaps most significantly, the latter years of Gandhi-Singh rule may have inflicted lasting damage to India's investment-growth potential for the foreseeable future.

---

13 December 2012.

38

India's Urbanisation Challenge

Half-way through its 40-page manifesto, the Bharatiya Janata Party (BJP), the likely anchor of a new coalition government, identifies 'urban areas' as 'high growth centres' for India's development and promises to build a '100 new cities'. The identification of good urban policies as prerequisites for rapid economic and social development is sound: two-third of national GDP (gross domestic product) comes from urban India. The apparent focus on new cities is not. What India needs is not a whole lot of very costly, brand new cities but a revamping of urban institutional structures and policies to improve the obvious squalor and inefficiencies of the country's existing 8,000 cities and towns. The BJP's brains trust on economic and social policies would do well to read three good new books on Indian urbanisation that have been published over the last two months.[1] They could start with Ahluwalia's highly readable and engaging introductory chapter to her book.

In this brief column, I rely heavily on these recent books to give some flavour of the major issues and challenges that India faces as her urbanisation proceeds. And proceed it will, since the shift from rural to urban habitation is an intrinsic dimension of the larger process of economic development and structural change experienced by all major nations. As incomes rise, the relative role of agriculture shrinks, while those of industry and services rise. And, the world over, these non-agricultural activities of industry and services prosper best in urban areas, which nurture the economies and efficiencies of scale, scope and connectedness (the so-called benefits of agglomeration). The choice before India is not whether or not to urbanise, but rather between

---

1. Ahluwalia, Isher (2014). *Transforming our Cities: Postcard of Change*. Harper Collins; Ahluwalia, Isher, Ravi Kanbur and P.K. Mohanty (eds.), (2014). *Urbanization in India*. Sage; and P.K. Mohanty (2014). *Cities and Public Policy*. Sage.

reasonably planned, efficient, growth-and employment-enhancing urbanisation and the higgledy-piggledy expansion of congested, polluted, under-serviced and unhealthy urban sprawls that are so typical of today's Indian urban landscape and so damaging to its long-term development prospects.

Some Dimensions of the Challenge

Actually, the pace of India's urbanisation has been slow by international standards. According to census and United Nations (UN) data, India's share of urban population in 2011 was 31.0 per cent as compared to around 50.0 per cent in China, Indonesia and Nigeria, 61 per cent in South Africa, 78.0 per cent in Mexico and 87.0 per cent in Brazil. In the 60 years from 1950 to 2011, India's urban population share rose from 17.0 per cent to 31.0 per cent, while China's quadrupled from 12.0 per cent to 49.0 per cent. Nevertheless, the number of people involved is large: in the 20 years from 1991 to 2011, India's urban population rose to 377 million, 160 million more than in 1991 and 90 million more than in 2001. By 2031, the urban population is projected to increase by over 200 million to 600 million, or 40 per cent of the national population.

Despite India's relatively low level and pace of urbanisation (by international standards), the condition of urban communities and their services in India is woefully inadequate. Consider the following:

- 25.0 per cent of urban India dwells in slums; in Greater Mumbai the ratio is over 50.0 per cent.

- Barring a couple of small towns in Maharashtra, no city provides continuous (24x7) piped water. And the water that does come, fitfully, is rarely fit to drink without boiling or other treatment. In contrast, cities in China and Brazil get much better water 24x7.

- Very few Indian towns (such as Chandigarh, Navi Mumbai and Surat) treat over 90.0 per cent of the sewage (excrement and waste water) before discharging them into rivers, sea and lakes. In the vast majority of urban communities treatment rates are far lower, well below 50.0 per cent. Until recently, it was 30.0 per cent in Delhi, now increased to 50 per cent.

- Urban India is estimated to produce 180,000 tonnes of garbage every day, most of which ends up in huge rubbish heaps or 'landhills', instead of being composted, converted to energy or sealed in sanitary landfills. Overflowing garbage bins and rubbish heaps are common sights.

- Little wonder that diseases like dengue, malaria, typhoid, swine flu, diarrhea and respiratory ailments are on the rise in most towns in India.

- Urban road systems are grossly inadequate and poorly maintained. Typically, public transport is scarce: only about 500 out of 8,000 cities and towns have a public bus system!

The Way Forward

At the heart of the quality of urbanisation is the governance system of institutions and policies that guide and oversee the planning, execution and coordination of land use, building regulations, road construction and delivery of key services such as water supply, sanitation, transport, and solid waste disposal, while ensuring adequate mobilisation of the necessary financial resources. The institutional framework for urbanisation in India has been historically weak. Significant improvement occurred in 1992 through the 74th Amendment to the Constitution, which emphasised the importance of ULBs (urban local bodies). But many believe that this matter needs to be revisited to assign better revenue resources to ULBs, clarify expenditure responsibilities in relation to state and central governments, and improve the staffing and competencies of these bodies.

Such systemic reform may well be necessary. But a great deal can be accomplished within the existing framework with strong administrative and legal support from state governments and some assistance from the centre, as through the Jawaharlal Nehru National Urban Renewal Mission. First, it is surely shocking that while over 2,000 new areas were designated as 'towns' by census enumerators (according to established criteria of population, density and employment in non-agriculture pursuits) between 2001 and 2011, the number of towns with statutory ULBs increased by less than 250. Thus a very large number of small towns do not have an ULB to deliver the basic services necessary to avail the benefits of agglomeration. The facilitation of new ULBs is surely a primary task of state governments, with some assistance from the centre.

Second, ULBs are chronically short of resources. Yet within the existing framework, many of them, especially city municipalities, could do a far better job in exploiting existing revenue bases such as the property tax. International comparisons show that Indian cities are unusually deficient in raising revenue from property taxes, usually the prime source of income for urban local governments worldwide. Indeed, as Mohanty spells out, there is a range of other revenue instruments which could be deployed for harnessing some of the soaring land values in urban locales in order to fund the necessary urban infrastructure. Third, user charges need to play a bigger role to fund provision of services such as water, electricity, bus services and waste disposal. Fourth, as Ahluwalia shows, ULBs can and have improved resource mobilisation and service provision through intelligent deployment of information technology. More generally, there is a great deal that India's urban governments can learn from each other. Ahluwalia documents some 40 case studies of progress in urban service provision. Not all of them are replicable or scalable. But quite a few surely are, especially with requisite support of state governments.

The basic point is simple. Well-functioning urban institutions and sound policies will nurture faster economic growth and more employment for the cities as well as the nation. Continued neglect of urban governance and policies could cost the nation dearly. And the focus has to be on India's 8,000 existing cities and towns, not on a few dozen costly new showpieces.

---

8 May 2014.

39

The National Development Policy Commission

Ever since the Prime Minister announced the demise of the Planning Commission (PC) from the ramparts of the Red Fort last month, the commentariat has been busy speculating about and pronouncing on the shape of the new institution to take its place. I feel duty-bound to offer some thoughts. My focus will be entirely on the new body, not on the erstwhile PC. All I will say on the latter is that I am broadly sympathetic to the fairly widespread view (see, for example, C. Rangarajan in the *Hindu* of 28 August 2014) that the PC's roles of financial resource allocation, project appraisal/evaluation and acting as a secretariat to the National Development Council can, and should be, transferred to other organs of the government, such as ministries and the Finance Commission. Its role of preparing medium-term blue prints (plans) for national economic and social development needs to be seriously recast before inclusion in the mandate of the successor institution.

So what should the new institution do? How should it be staffed? How should it be empowered? What should it be called?

Functions

Much of the commentary thus far has assumed that the new body should be some sort of government 'think tank' or 'think tank plus'. Well, yes, may be...except the connotation of 'think tank' to many people is of a research organisation primarily charged with undertaking basic or applied research, with the latter sometimes feeding into policy. My discomfort with this is that government organs in India too often dismiss think tanks (and their output) as 'academic', in the sense of not practically useful. I believe the intention here is much more about constituting a policy-focused organisation, which is charged with advising government (initially central, later including states which seek advice) on key policies of national economic and social development. Of course, to be credible and useful, such policy advice has to be analytically sound, research-based and cognizant of the real political economy. It should be backed by a good deal of 'creative thinking' to use the prime minister's phrase.

It would be unrealistic to expect the new institution to be able to credibly advise on all big issues in national development right away. Where should it start? My suggestion would be to initially build analytical/advisory capacity in four or five key priority areas indicated below.

- *International economic analysis*: we live in a fast-changing world, where shifts in economic power, trade, technology and capital flows are often quite swift, with serious implications for India's development potential, possibilities, constraints and policies. Yet no single place in the current government structure is well-equipped to assess these developments, draw out the implications for India and advise on appropriate national policy. The new institution is the right home.

- *Employment and labour markets*: Creating many more half-decent jobs for the 10 million plus new entrants to the labour force each year must surely constitute the primary development challenge for India today. Labour-using economic development is the surest path to greater 'inclusion' in our society, a path we have yet to find. The new institution should accord primary attention to understanding the primary constraints to employment-intensive development in today's India and then propagate the policy reforms required to lift these constraints.

- *Energy and environment*: As we know from a daily reading of newspapers, India faces major and complex issues in energy production, pricing, demand management, coordination/ planning across subsectors (coal, hydro, oil and gas, nuclear, electricity and solar and other non-conventional sources) and the associated issues relating to environmental impact and conservation. These issues need sustained, high quality analysis to yield good policies so as to develop the country's varied energy supplies to meet the growing demand.

- *Transport and communication*: Similarly, the domain of transport and communication development cuts across various sectors (such as railways, roads, ports, shipping, inland waterways, air transport, telecommunication, and information technology) and ministerial responsibilities. Here too, medium and long range forward thinking is critical to develop the right kind of development strategies and to foster appropriate regulatory and policy frameworks. As in the case of energy/environment, this set of issues needs urgent and continuous analytical attention, which the new institution should aim to provide.

- *Water, sanitation and public health*: Issues of water scarcity and mismanagement are becoming serious constraints to both rural and urban development. Water is linked to many things, including the long-festering problems of inadequate sanitation and sewerage, which are at last receiving serious attention, especially since they are closely linked to basic issues of public health. Again, because of the cross-sectoral (and cross-ministerial) nature of these problems, the new institution would do well to focus on this area early in its evolution.

What About a Name?

Names are important. Here's by suggestion: National Development Policy Commission (NDPC). That should make clear that the new institution is national, it's about development, and crucially, it's about actual government policy... that it's not just a think tank producing research papers only a few read. Of course, a name is no guarantee of a vibrant and effective future.

Organisation and Staffing

If the new NDPC is to get off to a good start, two things are absolutely essential. It must have strong prime ministerial support and must be equipped with high quality staff. As in the case of the erstwhile PC, the Prime Minister should chair the NDPC , with a well-empowered, cabinet-level deputy, who really runs the institution. Will that be enough to ensure that the rest of the government pays attention to the policy papers and advice offered by the NDPC, especially in the absence of the PC's allocative functions? That is an open question. There are ways of increasing the chances for getting governmental attention; such as by requiring cabinet discussion and decision on the policy papers prepared by the NDPC; or by requiring that all cabinet notes in the NDPC's designated (and gradually evolving) areas of focus/expertise should only reach the cabinet after inclusion of the NDPC's comments.

The effectiveness of the NDPC will depend crucially on the quality of its policy advice. And the best chance of ensuring high quality advice is to staff the organisation with high quality staff, whether economists, technologists or various domain experts. Ergo, the NDPC must have highly flexible recruitment rules, which allow engagement of high quality analysts for several years or a few months as required. Their number need not be large. It must also have a generous consultancy/research budget, which allows it to readily farm out necessary, specialised, studies to existing think tanks and non-government experts. It must not become a convenient parking spot for various 'surplus' government cadres.

Beyond all this, the NDPC's success (or failure) will depend on luck and the unknowable trajectory of events and people that actually make history.

---

11 September 2014.